Cambridge
BEC Vantage
1

REGENT'S UNIVERSITY LONDON | Park Campus Library

Examination papers from University of Cambridge ESOL Examinations: English for Speakers of Other Languages

REGENT'S UNIVERSITY LONDON WITHDRAWN

CAMBRIDGE UNIVERSITY PRESS

D1464109

REGENTS COLLEGE LIBRARY
17018685

CAMBRIDGE UNIVERSITY PRESS
Cambridge, New York, Melbourne, Madrid, Cape Town,
Singapore, São Paulo, Delhi, Tokyo, Mexico City

Cambridge University Press
The Edinburgh Building, Cambridge CB2 8RU, UK

Published in the United States of America by
Cambridge University Press, New York

www.cambridge.org
Information on this title: www.cambridge.org/9780521753043

© Cambridge University Press 2002

It is normally necessary for written permission for copying to be obtained *in advance*
from a publisher. The normal requirements are waived here and it is not necessary to
write to Cambridge University Press for permission for an individual teacher to
make copies for use within his or her own classroom. Only those pages which carry the
wording Photocopiable © UCLES may be copied.

This publication is in copyright. Subject to statutory exception
and to the provisions of relevant collective licensing agreements,
no reproduction of any part may take place without the written
permission of Cambridge University Press.

First published 2002
5th printing 2011

A catalogue record for this publication is available from the British Library

ISBN 978-0-521-75304-3 Student's Book with answers
ISBN 978-0-521-75305-0 Audio Cassette
ISBN 978-0-521-75306-7 Audio CD

Cambridge University Press has no responsibility for the persistence or
accuracy of URLs for external or third-party internet websites referred to in
this publication, and does not guarantee that any content on such websites is,
or will remain, accurate or appropriate. Information regarding prices, travel
timetables, and other factual information given in this work is correct at
the time of first printing but Cambridge University Press does not guarantee
the accuracy of such information thereafter.

REGENT'S COLLEGE
ACC No. 17012 685
CLASS 428.24076 UNI
S.I.
EY ENGLISH LANGUAGE -
EXAMINATIONS, QUESTIONS

Contents

Introduction

TO THE STUDENT

This book is for candidates preparing for the University of Cambridge Local Examinations Syndicate (UCLES) Business English Certificate Vantage Level examination. It contains four complete tests which reflect the most recent specifications (introduced in March 2002).

The BEC Suite

The Business English Certificates (BEC) are certificated examinations which can be taken on up to six fixed dates per year at approved Cambridge BEC centres. They are aimed primarily at individual learners who wish to obtain a business-related English language qualification and provide an ideal focus for courses in Business English. Set in a business context, BEC tests English language, not business knowledge. BEC is available at three levels – Preliminary, Vantage and Higher.

BEC Vantage

Within the three levels, BEC Vantage is at Cambridge Level 3.

Cambridge Level 4 BEC Higher
Cambridge Level 3 BEC Vantage
Cambridge Level 2 BEC Preliminary

The exam is based on the former Business English Certificate 2, which has been revised to keep pace with changes in business practice and language teaching and testing, and renamed.

The BEC Vantage examination consists of four papers:

Reading	1 hour
Writing	45 minutes
Listening	40 minutes (approximately)
Speaking	14 minutes

Test of Reading

This paper consists of five parts with 45 questions, which take the form of two multiple matching tasks, two multiple choice tasks, and an error identification task. Part 1 contains four short texts or a longer text divided into four sections, and Parts 2, 3, 4 and 5 each contain one longer text. The texts are taken from newspapers, business magazines, business correspondence, books, leaflets, brochures, etc. They are all business related, and are selected to test a wide range of reading skills and strategies.

Test of Writing

For this paper, candidates are required to produce two pieces of writing. For Part 1, they write a note, message, memo or email to a colleague or colleagues within the company. For Part 2, they write a piece of business correspondence to somebody outside the company, a short report or a proposal.

Candidates are asked to write 40 to 50 words for Part 1 and 120 to 140 words for Part 2. Assessment is based on achievement of task, range and accuracy of vocabulary and grammatical structures, organisation, content and appropriacy of register and format.

Test of Listening

This paper consists of three parts with 30 questions, which take the form of a note completion task, a multiple choice task and a further multiple choice task. Part 1 contains three short conversations, Part 2 contains ten very short extracts, and Part 3 contains one longer text. The texts are audio-recordings based on a variety of sources including interviews, telephone calls, face to face conversations and documentary features. They are all business related, and are selected to test a wide range of listening skills and strategies.

Test of Speaking

The Speaking Test consists of three parts, which take the form of an interview section, a short talk on a business topic, and a discussion. Candidates are examined in pairs by two examiners, an Interlocutor and an Assessor. The Assessor awards a mark based on the following four criteria: Grammar and Vocabulary, Discourse Management, Pronunciation and Interactive Communication. The Interlocutor provides a global mark for the whole test.

Marks and results

The three BEC Vantage papers total 120 marks, after weighting. Each paper is weighted to 30 marks. A candidate's overall grade is based on the total score gained in all four papers. It is not necessary to achieve a satisfactory level in all four papers in order to pass the examination. Pass grades are A, B and C, with A being the highest. D and E are failing grades. Every candidate is provided with a Statement of Results which includes a graphical display of their performance in each paper. These are shown against the scale Exceptional – Good – Borderline – Weak and indicate the candidate's relative performance in each paper.

TO THE TEACHER

Candidature

Each year BEC is taken by over 50,000 candidates throughout the world. Most candidates are either already in work or studying in preparation for the world of work.

Content, preparation and assessment

Material used throughout BEC is as far as possible authentic and free of bias, and reflects the international flavour of the examination. The subject matter should not advantage or disadvantage certain groups of candidates, nor should it offend in areas such as religion, politics or sex.

TEST OF READING

PART	MAIN SKILL FOCUS	Input: Text type, content	Response	No. of Items /marks
1	Reading – scanning and gist	One longer or four shorter informational texts (approx. 250–350 words in total)	Matching	7
2	Reading – understanding text structure	Single text: article, report, etc. with sentence level gaps (text plus 7 option sentences approx. 450–550 words in total)	Matching	5
3	Reading for gist and specific information	Single text (approx. 450–550 words)	4-option multiple choice	6
4	Reading – vocabulary and structure information	Single informational text with lexical gaps (text including gapped words approx. 200–300 words)	4-option multiple choice cloze	15
5	Reading – understanding sentence structure / error identification	Short text (150–200 words) Identification of additional unnecessary words in text	Proof reading	12

Reading Part One

This is a matching task. There are four short texts on a related theme (for example descriptions of a group of products, or advertisements for jobs) or a single text divided into four sections. Although the context of each text will be similar, there will also be information that is particular to each text. The texts are labelled A–D. Candidates are presented with a set of seven items which are statements related to the texts. They are expected to match each statement with the relevant text. Questions in this part tend to focus mostly on the identification of specific information and detail. However, an item could focus on gist by testing areas such as the target reader or the topic.

Preparation
In order to prepare for this part it would be useful to familiarise students with sets of short texts that have a similar theme. Newspapers, magazines and catalogues are useful sources in which to find such texts. Students should be encouraged to look closely at all the information, particularly as short texts often include additional snippets of information on separate lines (such as prices, dates, titles, measurements, etc.) that can easily be overlooked.

Students could be set questions which test global reading skills prior to reading the texts, so that they are trained to think automatically of who a text is written for and why it has been written.

Reading Part Two

This is a matching task, comprising a text that has had six sentences removed from it and a set of seven sentences labelled A–G. Candidates are required to match each gap with the sentence which they think fits in terms of meaning and structure. The first gap is always given as an example so that candidates have five gaps left to complete. When they have finished this part there will be one sentence left which they have not used.

The texts for this part will have been chosen because they have a clear line of thought or argument that can still be discerned by the reader with the sentences removed. In doing the task, therefore, students should be trained to read through the gapped text and the list of sentences first, in order to get an idea of what it is about. Having done that, they should be reassured that there is only one sentence that fits each gap.

This part is a test of text structure as well as meaning and the gaps will be reasonably far apart so that candidates can successfully anticipate the appropriate lexical and grammatical features of the missing sentence. Candidates can be expected to be tested on a variety of cohesive features with both a backward and forward reference, sometimes going beyond the sentence level. Thus, while selecting the appropriate sentence for a gap, they should read before and after the text to ensure that it fits well. At the end of this part, they should read through the entire text, inserting the gapped sentences as they go along, to ensure that the information is coherent.

Preparation
This can be quite a difficult task, especially for candidates who are unfamiliar with such an exercise. In preparing them for this part, it would be a good idea to select a number of graded texts that have clear, familiar ideas and evident cohesive features. Texts can be cut up as they are in the test or simply discussed in their entirety. In this way, students can work up to dealing with more complex material and identifying the many different ways that ideas are connected. It would also be useful when doing gapped texts to look at sentences that do not fit in gaps and discuss the reasons for this. Sometimes it is possible to make a sentence fit a gap by simply changing a few words. Discussion on areas such as this would also be fruitful.

Reading Part Three

This task consists of a text accompanied by four-option multiple choice items. The stem of a multiple choice item may take the form of a question or an incomplete sentence. There are six items, which are placed after the text. The text is 450 to 550 words long. Sources of original texts may be the general and business press, company literature and books on topics such as management. Texts may be edited, but the source is authentic.

Preparation
- multiple choice questions are a familiar and long-standing type of test; here they are used to test opinion and inference rather than straightforward facts;
- correct answers are not designed to depend on simple word-matching, and students' ability to interpret paraphrasing should be developed;
- students should be encouraged to pursue their own interpretation of relevant parts of the text and then check their idea against the options offered, rather than reading all the options first;
- it could be useful for students to be given perhaps one of the wrong options only, and for them to try to write the correct answer and another wrong option.

Reading Part Four

This is a multiple choice cloze test with fifteen gaps, most of which test lexical items, and may focus on correct word choice, lexical collocations and fixed phrases. The texts chosen for this part will come from varied sources but they will all have a straightforward message or meaning, so that candidates are being tested on vocabulary and not on their comprehension of the passage.

Preparation
Candidates are usually familiar with this type of task and so it is most important to try and improve their range of vocabulary. The options provided in each item in the test will have similar meanings but only one word will be correct within the context provided. Familiarity with typical collocations would be especially useful. The language of business is often very precise and so it is worth spending time looking at the vocabulary used in different types of text, getting students to keep a vocabulary list and encouraging them to make active use of the lexical items that are new to them.

Reading Part Five

This is an error-correction or proof-reading task based on a text of 150 to 200 words, with twelve items. Candidates identify additional or unnecessary words in a text. This task can be related to the authentic task of checking a text for errors, and suitable text types are therefore letters, publicity materials, etc. The text is presented with twelve numbered lines, which are the lines containing the items. Further lines at the end may complete the text, but they are not numbered.

Preparation
- students should be reminded that this task represents a kind of editing that is common practice, even in their first language;
- any work on error analysis is likely to be helpful for this task;
- it may well be that photocopies of students' own writing could provide an authentic source for practice;
- a reverse of the exercise (giving students texts with missing words) might prove beneficial.

Marks

One mark is given for each correct answer. The total score is then weighted to 30 marks for the whole Reading paper.

TEST OF WRITING

PART	Functions/Communicative Task	Input	Response	Register
1	e.g. giving instructions, explaining a development, asking for comments, requesting information, agreeing to requests	Rubric only (plus layout of output text type)	Internal communication (medium may be note or message or memo or email (40–50 words)	Neutral/ informal
2	Correspondence: e.g. explaining, apologising, reassuring, complaining Report: describing, summarising Proposal: describing, summarising, recommending, persuading	One or more pieces of input from: business correspondence (medium may be letter, fax or email), internal communication (medium may be note, memo or email) notice, advert, graphs, charts, etc. (plus layout if output is fax or email)	Business correspondence (medium may be letter or fax or email) or short report or proposal (medium may be memo or email) email (120–140 words)	Neutral/ formal

For BEC Vantage, candidates are required to produce two pieces of writing:
- an internal company communication; this means a piece of communication with a colleague or colleagues within the company on a business-related matter, and the delivery medium may be a note, message, memo or email;
- and one of the following:
  - a piece of business correspondence; this means correspondence with somebody outside the company (e.g. a customer or supplier) on a business-related matter, and the delivery medium may be letter, fax or email;
  - a report; this means the presentation of information in relation to a specific issue or events. The report will contain an introduction, main body of findings and conclusion; it is possible that the delivery medium may be a memo or an email;
  - a proposal; this has a similar format to a report, but unlike the report, the focus of the proposal is on the future, with the main focus being on recommendations for discussion; it is possible that the delivery medium may be a memo or an email.

Writing Part One

In the first task candidates are presented with the context in the task rubric. This explains the role the candidate must take in order to write a note, message, memo or email of around 40 to 50 words using a written prompt. It also identifies who the message is to be written to. The prompt will be included in the instructions in the rubric and will be in the form of bullet points clearly stating the pieces of information that must be incorporated into the answer.

Writing Part Two

In the second Writing task, candidates are required to write 120 to 140 words, which will be in the form of business correspondence, a short report or proposal. There will be an explanation of the task and one or more texts as input material. These texts may contain visual or graphic material, and have 'hand-written' notes on them.

Preparing for the Writing questions

Students should have practice in the clear and concise presentation of written information. Exposure to, and discussion of, as wide a range as possible of relevant texts would be beneficial. Students should be trained to consider:
- the target reader
- references to previous communication
- the purpose of writing
- the requirements of the format (e.g. letter, report)
- the main points to be addressed
- the approximate number of words to be written for each point
- suitable openings and closings
- the level of formality required.

It is important that students are aware of the need to reformulate the wording of the content points/handwritten notes given in the task, in order to include original vocabulary and structures, since evidence of a range of structures and vocabulary is one of the marking criteria.

Assessment

An impression mark is awarded to each piece of writing using the general mark scheme. Examiners use band descriptors to assess language and task achievement. Each piece of writing is assigned to a band between 0 and 5 and can be awarded one of two performance levels within that band. Acceptable performance at BEC Vantage level is represented by Band 3.

The general impression mark scheme is used in conjunction with a task-specific mark scheme, which focuses on content, range of structures, vocabulary, organisation, register and format and the effect on the target reader of a specific task.

American spelling and usage is acceptable.

The band scores awarded are translated to a mark out of 10 for Part 1 and a mark out of 20 for Part 2.

General mark scheme – Writing

Band		Part 1 Mark	Part 2 Mark
5	Full realisation of the task set. • All content points included and expanded upon where the task allows. • Controlled, natural use of language; minimal errors which are minor. • Wide range of structure and vocabulary. • Effectively organised, with appropriate use of cohesive devices. • Register and format consistently appropriate. Very positive effect on the reader.	9 or 10	18 or 20
4	Good realisation of the task set. • All content points adequately dealt with. • Generally accurate; errors when complex language is attempted. • Good range of structure and vocabulary. • Generally well-organised, with attention paid to cohesion. • Register and format on the whole appropriate. Positive effect on the reader.	7 or 8	14 or 16
3	Reasonable achievement of the task set. • All major content points included; some minor omissions • A number of errors will be present, but they do not impede communication. • Adequate range of structure and vocabulary. • Organisation and cohesion is satisfactory, on the whole. • Register and format reasonable, although not entirely successful. Satisfactory effect on the reader.	5 or 6	10 or 12
2	Inadequate attempt at the task set. • Some major content points omitted or inadequately dealt with; some irrelevance is likely. • Errors sometimes obscure communication, are numerous, and distract the reader. • Limited range of structure and vocabulary. • Content is not clearly organised or linked, causing some confusion. • Inappropriate register and format. Negative effect on the reader.	3 or 4	6 or 8
1	Poor attempt at the task set. • Notable content omissions and / or considerable irrelevance, possibly due to misinterpretation of the task set. • Serious lack of control; frequent basic errors. • Little evidence of structure and vocabulary required by task. • Lack of organisation, causing a breakdown in communication. • Little attempt at appropriate register and format. Very negative effect on the reader.	1 or 2	2 or 4
0	Achieves nothing. Either fewer than 25% of the required number of words or totally illegible or totally irrelevant.	0	0

TEST OF LISTENING

PART	MAIN SKILL FOCUS	Input	Item type	No. of Items
1	Listening for writing short answers	Three telephone conversations or messages	Gap filling	12
2	Listening; identifying topic, context, function, etc.	Short monologue; two sections of five 'snippets' each	Multiple matching	10
3	Listening	One extended conversation or monologue; interview, discussion, presentation, etc.	Multiple choice	8

Listening Part One

In this part there are three conversations or answering machine messages, with a gapped text to go with each. Each gapped text provides a very clear context and has four spaces which have to be filled with one or two words or a number. The gapped texts may include forms, diary excerpts, invoices, message pads, etc. Candidates hear each conversation or message twice and as they listen they are required to complete the gapped text.

This part of the Listening test concentrates on the retrieval of factual information and it is important for candidates to listen carefully using the prompts on their question paper in order to identify the missing information. For example, they may have to note down a person's name, and if names on the tape are spelt out, those answers must be spelt correctly. Alternatively, they may have to listen for a room or telephone number, or an instruction or deadline. Answers to this part are rarely a simple matter of dictation and some reformulation of the prompt material will be required in order to locate the correct answer.

Listening Part Two

This part is divided into two sections. Each section has the same format: candidates hear five short monologues and have to match each monologue to a set of items A–H. In each section, the eight options will form a coherent set and the overall theme or topic will be clearly stated in the task rubric. For example, candidates may hear five people talking and have to decide what sort of jobs the people do. Hence the set of options A–H will contain a list of jobs. Alternatively the set of options may consist of eight places/topics/addressees/ purposes, etc. The two sections will always test different areas and so if the first section focuses on say, topics, the second section will focus on something else, such as functions.

In this part of the Listening test, candidates are being tested on their global listening skills and also on their ability to infer, extract gist and understand main ideas. In order to answer the questions successfully, they will need to work out the answer by developing ideas, and refining these as the text is heard. It will not be possible to 'word match' and candidates should not expect to hear such overt clues. However, there will always be a 'right' answer and candidates are not expected to opt for the 'best' answer.

Listening Part Three

A longer text is heard in this part, usually lasting approximately four minutes. The text will typically be an interview, conversation or discussion with two or more speakers, or possibly a presentation or report with one speaker. There are eight, three-option multiple choice questions that focus on details and main ideas in the text. There may be questions on opinions and feelings but these will be relatively straightforward and will not require candidates to remember long or complex pieces of information.

Preparing for the Listening Paper

All listening practice should be helpful for students, whether authentic or specially prepared. In particular, discussion should focus on:
- the purpose of speeches and conversations or discussions;
- the role of speakers'
- the opinions expressed;
- the language functions employed;
- relevant aspects of phonology such as stress, linking and weak forms, etc.
  In addition, students should be encouraged to appreciate the differing demands of each task type. It will be helpful not only to practise the task types in order to develop a sense of familiarity and confidence, but also to discuss how the three task types relate to real life skills and situations:
- the first is note-taking (and therefore productive), and students should reflect on the various situations in which they take notes from a spoken input. They should also be encouraged to try to predict the kinds of words or numbers that might go in the gaps;
- the second is a matching (with discrimination) exercise, and reflects the ability to interrelate information between reading and listening and across differing styles and registers;
- the third involves the correct interpretation of spoken input, with correct answers often being delivered across different speakers.
  In all three tasks, successful listening depends on correct reading, and students should be encouraged to make full use of the pauses during the test to check the written input.

Marks

One mark is given for each correct answer, giving a total score of 30 marks for the whole Listening paper.

TEST OF SPEAKING

PART	Format and Focus	Time	Candidate Focus
1	Conversation between the interlocutor and each candidate Giving personal information. Talking about present circumstances, past experiences and future plans, expressing opinions, speculating, etc.	About 3 minutes	The interlocutor encourages the candidates to give information about themselves and to express personal opinions
2	A 'mini presentation' by each candidate on a business theme Organising a larger unit of discourse. Giving information and expressing and justifying opinions	About 6 minutes	The candidates are given prompts which generate a short talk on a business-related topic
3	Two-way conversation between candidates followed by further prompting from the interlocutor Expressing and justifying opinions, speculating, comparing and contrasting agreeing and disagreeing, etc.	About 5 minutes	The candidates are presented with a discussion on a business-related topic The interlocutor extends the discussion with prompts on related topics

The Speaking Test is conducted by two Oral Examiners (an Interlocutor and an Assessor), with pairs of candidates. The Interlocutor is responsible for conducting the Speaking Test and is also required to give a mark for each candidate's performance during the whole test. The Assessor is responsible for providing an analytical assessment of each candidate's performance and, after being introduced by the Interlocutor, takes no further part in the interaction.

The Speaking Test is designed for pairs of candidates. However, where a centre has an uneven number of candidates, the last three candidates will be examined together. Oral Examiner packs contain shared tasks which are particularly appropriate for these groups of three.

Speaking Part One

In the first part of the test, the interlocutor addresses each candidate in turn and asks general questions. Candidates will not be addressed in strict sequence. This part of the test lasts about 3 minutes and during this time, candidates are being tested on their ability to talk about themselves: to provide personal information on their home, interests and jobs, and to perform functions such as agreeing and disagreeing, and expressing preferences.

Speaking Part Two

The second part of the test is a 'mini presentation'. In this part the candidates are given a choice of topic and about one minute to prepare a piece of extended speech. After each candidate has spoken their partner will be invited to ask a question about what has been said.

Speaking Part Three

The third part of the test is a two-way conversation (three-way in a three candidate format) between candidates. The interlocutor gives candidates a topic to discuss. The candidates are asked to speak for about 3 minutes. The interlocutor will support the conversation as appropriate and then ask further questions related to the main theme.

Preparing for the Speaking test

It is important to familiarise candidates with the format of the test before it takes place, by the use of paired activities in class. Teachers may need to explain the benefits of this type of assessment to candidates. The primary purpose of paired assessment is to sample a wider range of discourse than can be elicited from an individual interview. In the first part of the test, candidates mainly respond to questions or comments from the interlocutor.

Students need practice in exchanging personal and non-personal information; at Vantage level it may be possible for students to practise talking about themselves in pairs with or without prompts (such as written questions). However, prompt materials are necessary for Parts Two and Three, and students could be encouraged to design these themselves or may be provided with specially prepared sets. In small classes, students could discuss authentic materials as a group prior to engaging in pairwork activities. Such activities familiarise students with the types of interactive skills involved in asking and providing factual information such as: speaking clearly, formulating questions, listening carefully and giving precise answers.

In the 'mini presentation' candidates are being asked to show an ability to talk for an extended period of time. Discussion activities as well as giving short talks or presentation should help to develop this skill.

In the final discussion in the Vantage Speaking test, candidates are also being tested on their ability to express opinions, to compare and contrast, to concede points and possibly to reach a conclusion (although it is perfectly acceptable for candidates to agree to differ). Any discussion activities on a business theme that encourage students to employ these skills will be beneficial. Group or class discussions are valuable ways of developing these skills.

Assessment

Candidates are assessed on their own performance and not in relation to each other according to the following analytical criteria; Grammar and Vocabulary, Discourse Management, Pronunciation and Interactive Communication. These criteria are interpreted at Vantage level. Assessment is based on performance in the whole test and is not related to particular parts of the test.

Both examiners assess the candidates. The Assessor applies detailed, analytical scales, and the Interlocutor applies a global achievement scale which is based on the analytical scales. The analytical criteria are further described below:

Grammar and Vocabulary

This refers to range and accuracy as well as the appropriate use of grammatical and lexical forms. At BEC Vantage level a range of grammar and vocabulary is needed to deal with the tasks. At this level candidates should be accurate enough, and use sufficiently appropriate vocabulary, to convey their intended meanings.

Discourse Management

This refers to the coherence, extent and relevance of each candidate's individual performance. Contributions should be adequate to deal with the BEC Vantage level tasks. At times, candidates' utterances may be inappropriate in length.

Pronunciation

This refers to the candidate's ability to produce comprehensible utterances. At BEC Vantage level, meanings are conveyed through the appropriate use of stress, rhythm, intonation and clear individual sounds, although there may be occasional difficulty for the listener.

Interactive Communication

This refers to the candidate's ability to take an active part in the development of the discourse. At BEC Vantage level, candidates should be sensitive to turn taking and sustain the interaction by initiating and responding appropriately. Hesitation may, at times, demand patience of the listener.

Global Achievement Scale

This refers to the candidate's overall performance throughout the test.

Throughout the Speaking Test candidates are assessed on their language skills and in order to be able to make a fair and accurate assessment of each candidate's performance, the examiners must be given an adequate sample of language to assess. Candidates must, therefore, be prepared to provide full answers to the questions asked by either the Interlocutor or the other candidate, and to speak clearly and audibly. While it is the responsibility of the Interlocutor, where necessary, to manage or direct the interaction, thus ensuring that both candidates are given an equal opportunity to speak, it is the responsibility of the candidates to maintain the interaction as much as possible. Candidates who take equal turns in the interchange will utilise to best effect the amount of time available.

Grading and results

Grading takes place once all scripts have been returned to UCLES and marking is complete. This is approximately five weeks after the examination. There are two main stages: grading and awards.

Grading

The four papers total 120 marks, after weighting. Each skill represents 25% of the total marks available.

The grade boundaries (A, B, C, D and E) are set using the following information:

- statistics on the candidature
- statistics on the overall candidate performance
- statistics on individual items, for those parts of the examination for which this is appropriate (Reading and Listening)
- the advice of the Chief Examiners, based on the performance of candidates, and on the recommendation of examiners where this is relevant (Writing)
- comparison with statistics from previous years' examination performance and candidature.

A candidate's overall grade is based on the total score gained in all three papers. It is not necessary to achieve a satisfactory level in all three papers in order to pass the examination.

Awards

The Awarding Committee deals with all cases presented for special consideration, e.g. temporary disability, unsatisfactory examination conditions, suspected collusion, etc. The committee can decide to ask for scripts to be re-marked, to check results, to change grades, to withhold results, etc. Results may be withheld because of infringement of regulations or because further investigation is needed. Centres are notified if a candidate's results have been scrutinised by the Awarding Committee.

Results

Results are reported as three passing grades (A, B and C) and two failing grades (D and E). Candidates are given statements of results which, in addition to their grades, show a graphical profile of their performance on each paper. These are shown against the scale Exceptional – Good – Borderline – Weak and indicate the candidate's relative performance in each paper. Certificates are issued to passing candidates after the issue of statements of results and there is no limit on the validity of the certificate.

Further information

For more information about BEC or any other UCLES examination write to:
EFL Information
University of Cambridge Local Examinations Syndicate
1 Hills Road
Cambridge
CB1 2EU
United Kingdom

Tel: +44 1223 553355
Fax: +44 1223 460278
email: efl@ucles.org.uk
www.cambridge-efl.org.uk
In some areas, this information can also be obtained from the British Council.

Test 1

READING   1 hour

READING

READING

PART ONE

Questions 1–7

- Look at the statements below and the company news reports on the opposite page.
- Which news report (**A**, **B**, **C** or **D**) does each statement **1–7** refer to?
- For each sentence **1–7**, mark one letter (**A**, **B**, **C**, or **D**) on your Answer Sheet.
- You will need to use some of the letters more than once.

Example:

0   This company is going to reduce staff numbers.

---

1 A strong currency has had a negative effect on the company.

2 The workforce has made it difficult for this company to become more efficient.

3 The use of specialists led to very high costs.

4 Increased competition has contributed to this company's difficulties.

5 This company has reached an agreement on a new project.

6 Part of this company was up for sale.

7 This company has expanded its manufacturing base.

A

Walger, the bus maker, has entered into a joint venture with IMCO Bus Corporation to participate in coachbuilding operations in Mexico. The two companies have just announced the $70 million acquisition of Mexican Coachworks, the largest bus and coach builder in Mexico, with 2,400 employees and three factories. Walger retains a 60% interest in the coachbuilding venture. Analysts have expressed surprise, given the current exchange rate.

B

Jetline Airports has said that it spent £2.1 million on its failed attempt to dispose of its duty-free retail division. The chief executive said the company's six-month search for a buyer ran up heavy consultancy expenses which left half-year pre-tax profits at £4.5 million. It also emerged that the Director of Finance received a £500,000 settlement when he left the company.

C

GRD, the manufacturing giant, plans to cut 1,500 jobs at its Portland factory over the next five years after union refusal to increase productivity. A company representative said that although they have invested more than $42 million in the new plant and improved technology, the trade unions are still unwilling to increase output. As a result, GRD have been forced to downsize the Portland plant.

D

Maybrooke, the Scottish department store, reported a fall in trading profits in the first half of the year from £545,000 to £462,000, on sales which were down two per cent. They blame the disappointing first half on the strength of the pound, which hit the company's tourist business, as well as an increase in traffic and parking problems in the city centre, and the growth of out-of-town shopping centres.

PART TWO

Questions 8–12

- Read the article below about changes in working hours.
- Choose the best sentence from the opposite page to fill in each of the gaps.
- For each gap **8–12**, mark one letter (**A–G**) on your Answer Sheet.
- Do not use any letter more than once.
- There is an example at the beginning (**0**).

GETTING THE BEST FROM YOUR STAFF

Ed Smith, a senior manager for Trustco Ltd in Worcester, used to work a minimum of 70 hours a week. He travelled regularly between the UK and USA and began to feel he had become almost a stranger to his wife and his two young sons. (**0**) ....*G*........ . This idea worked.

These days, he still goes to work very early but he also leaves early. He now sees his children before they go to bed and then does about an hour's work by computer from home in the evening, keeping in touch with American colleagues. (**8**).................. . The key to Ed Smith's changing his hours was persuading his employer that he and other staff were more productive when they worked the hours that suited them. This is easier said than done, of course. (**9**).................. . Many of them are slow to realise the benefits of letting employees work fewer or more flexible hours.

A recent survey of five thousand senior managers found that nearly half of them always worked more than their contract hours, while many worked evenings and weekends. A majority thought that this not only had a negative effect on their family relationships and their health, but also reduced their productivity. (**10**).................. . It seems that it is job satisfaction that is the deciding factor when it comes to employee productivity.

However, the good news is that more employers are now starting to realise that they are only going to get higher output from their staff if those staff are happy and want to be at work. (**11**).................. . His company have brought in changes partly for competitive reasons. The research and development part of the business employs highly trained scientists, who are expensive to replace. (**12**).................. . The employees seem to be very happy with the new arrangements and, as a result, productivity rates have gradually but consistently increased and staff turnover rates have fallen dramatically. According to Ed Smith, many companies would benefit from a similar scheme, and everyone, from directors to employees' families, would have something to gain.

Example: **0**

A Ed Smith's new working hours are just one example of the attempt to alter corporate culture.

B This adds to the increasing evidence that long hours are not necessarily useful hours.

C They are often willing to accept that happy employees produce more.

D He admits to feeling much happier, and believes he has established a balance between work and home life.

E It can be difficult to persuade organisations that a change of this type is in their interest, too.

F To keep them happy, 'trust time' has been introduced, where the company trusts employees to do what is required, in whatever time it takes.

G Realising that he was putting himself under too much stress, he decided to try to change his working hours.

PART THREE

Questions 13–18

- Read the article below about exporting and the questions on the opposite page.
- For each question **13–18**, mark one letter (**A, B, C** or **D**) on your Answer Sheet, for the answer you choose.

PROBLEMS FACING POTENTIAL EXPORTERS

Many firms fail because when they begin exporting they have not researched the target markets or developed an international marketing plan. To be successful, a firm must clearly define goals, objectives and potential problems. Secondly, it must develop a definitive plan to accomplish its objective, regardless of the problems involved. Unless the firm is fortunate enough to possess a staff with considerable expertise, it may not be able to take this crucial first step without qualified outside guidance.

Often top management is not committed enough to overcome the initial difficulties and financial requirements of exporting. It can often take more time and effort to establish a firm in a foreign market than in the domestic one. Although the early delays and costs involved in exporting may seem difficult to justify when compared to established domestic trade, the exporter should take a more objective view of this process and carefully monitor international marketing efforts through these early difficulties. If a good foundation is laid for export business, the benefits derived should eventually outweigh the investment.

Another problem area is in the selection of the foreign distributor. The complications involved in overseas communications and transportation require international distributors to act with greater independence than their domestic counterparts. Also, since a new exporter's trademarks and reputation are usually unknown in the foreign market, foreign customers may buy on the strength of the distributing agent's reputation. A firm should therefore conduct a thorough evaluation of the distributor's facilities, the personnel handling its account, and the management methods employed.

Another common difficulty for the new exporter is the neglect of the export market once the domestic one booms: too many companies only concentrate on exporting when there is a recession. Others may refuse to modify products to meet the regulations or cultural preferences of other countries. Local safety regulations cannot be ignored by exporters. If necessary modifications are not made at the factory, the distributor must make them, usually at a greater cost and probably not as satisfactorily. It should also be noted that the resulting smaller profit margin makes the account less attractive.

If exporters expect distributing agents to actively promote their accounts, they must be trained, and their performance continually monitored. This requires a company marketing executive to be located permanently in the distributor's geographical region. It is therefore advisable for new exporters to concentrate their efforts in a few geographical areas until there is sufficient business to support a company representative. The distributor should also be treated on an equal basis with domestic counterparts. For example, special discount offers, sales incentive programmes and special credit terms should be available.

Considering a joint-venture or licensing agreement is another option for new exporters. However, many companies still dismiss international marketing as unviable. There are a number of reasons for this. There may be import restrictions in the target market, the company may lack sufficient financial resources, or its product line may be too limited. Yet, many products that can compete on a national basis can be successful in the majority of world markets. In general, all that is needed for success is flexibility in using the proper combinations of marketing techniques.

13 In the first paragraph, the writer suggests that firms thinking about exporting should

    A   get professional advice.
    B   study international marketing.
    C   identify the most profitable markets.
    D   have different objectives to other exporters.

14 The writer believes that if sufficient preparation is undertaken

    A   initial difficulties can be easily avoided.
    B   the costs can be recovered quite quickly.
    C   management will become more committed.
    D   the exporter will be successful in the long term.

15 An exporter should choose a distributor who

    A   has experienced personnel.
    B   has good communication skills.
    C   is well-established in the target market.
    D   is not financially dependent on the import business.

16 New exporters often make the mistake of ignoring the export market when

    A   distribution costs are too high.
    B   their product is selling well at home.
    C   there is a global economic recession.
    D   distributors cannot make safety modifications.

17 For a distributor to be successful, the exporter must

    A   focus on one particular region.
    B   finance local advertising campaigns.
    C   give the same support as to domestic agents.
    D   make sure there are sufficient marketing staff locally.

18 In the last paragraph, the writer states that some companies are reluctant to export because

    A   there is little demand for their products.
    B   the importation of certain goods is controlled.
    C   they do not have good marketing techniques.
    D   they are not able to compete with local businesses.

PART FOUR

Questions 19–33

- Read the article below about a successful printing firm.
- Choose the best word to fill each gap, from **A**, **B**, **C** or **D** on the opposite page.
- For each question **19–33**, mark one letter (**A**, **B**, **C** or **D**) on your Answer Sheet.
- There is an example at the beginning (**0**).

MULTICOPY PRINTING

Martin Charlesworth pays a visit to discover the
(0) ......D...... of success at a busy printing firm.

From designing and printing corporate brochures and business cards to photocopying students' essays it's all in a day's work for Multicopy Printing. The family-run firm is one of the most successful printing, copyshop and design offices in the region. Although it is a (**19**).................. small company, it thinks big. The company has made a considerable (**20**).................. in high-tech machinery to (**21**).................. up in this rapidly changing industry.

The company's success has recently enabled it to modernise and (**22**).................. its premises. Multicopy's Managing Director, Colin Marsh, says, 'It was very (**23**).................. before. We may get up to two tonnes of paper delivered a day and we were running out of space to (**24**).................. it. Now, we're the only business in this area (**25**).................. a print service from start to finish all under one roof. A vast amount of work can be (**26**).................. in a very short space of time.'

The firm was (**27**).................. up 22 years ago by Colin's father, who was the area manager for a national (**28**).................. of printers before deciding to go into business on his own. In those days, it was mostly small printing (**29**).................. such as letter-heads and photocopying. The business grew rapidly in the mid-1980s with the (**30**).................. of new technology. Nowadays the core photocopying business is high-volume, sometimes up to 300,000 copies for one job, and it often needs to meet (**31**).................. deadlines for commercial outlets. But despite Multicopy's recent success, it has not forgotten its (**32**).................., and part of the everyday (**33**).................. still consists of doing small numbers of photocopies for members of the general public.

Example:

A key   **B** answer   **C** recipe   **D** secret

0	A	B	C	D
	▢	▢	▢	▬

19 **A** relatively   **B** roughly   **C** wholly   **D** nearly

20 **A** investment   **B** expense   **C** cost   **D** payment

21 **A** go   **B** get   **C** keep   **D** bring

22 **A** boost   **B** exceed   **C** continue   **D** expand

23 **A** closed   **B** crowded   **C** occupied   **D** filled

24 **A** reserve   **B** collect   **C** store   **D** fetch

25 **A** lending   **B** providing   **C** stocking   **D** holding

26 **A** settled   **B** built   **C** constructed   **D** completed

27 **A** taken   **B** put   **C** made   **D** set

28 **A** branch   **B** chain   **C** system   **D** series

29 **A** duties   **B** actions   **C** jobs   **D** labours

30 **A** event   **B** opening   **C** occasion   **D** introduction

31 **A** narrow   **B** sharp   **C** tight   **D** steep

32 **A** origins   **B** reasons   **C** bases   **D** causes

33 **A** duty   **B** routine   **C** method   **D** effort

PART FIVE

Questions 34–45

- Read the job advertisement below.
- In most of the lines **34–45**, there is one extra word. It is either grammatically incorrect or does not fit in with the meaning of the text. Some lines, however, are correct.
- If a line is correct, write **CORRECT** on your Answer Sheet.
- If there is an extra word in the line, write **the extra word** in CAPITAL LETTERS on your Answer Sheet.

Examples:

0	C	O	R	R	E	C	T	
00	T	O						

FOOD TECHNOLOGISTS REQUIRED

0   For all the diversity of the people who work at WP Foods, there is one

00 single thing that unites to us all: a passion to create something special

34 and a determination to be the best in whatever we do. We've been

35 producing high-quality foods for over than a century, and we travel to the

36 ends of all the earth to create the next generation of foods and drinks so

37 as to give delight our millions of customers. And thanks to our dedicated

38 staff, our much-loved brands just keep getting on better. We are now

39 seeking to appoint as innovators to manage a number of new teams in

40 the organisation. Applicants must have qualified a research degree in

41 Food Technology plus at least four years' industrial experience. We

42 need people with a high level of their team spirit who show themselves

43 be capable of explaining technical concepts to non-technical people.

44 Those appointed will spend significant amounts of time in other countries

45 for seeking new ingredients, but will also have a major influence on

    change throughout the business.

WRITING   45 minutes

WRITING

PART ONE

- You are the training manager of a company which has won a large export order. You have been asked to organise foreign language training for some of your staff.
- Write a **memo** to staff:
  - explaining why the courses are necessary
  - saying which members of staff should attend
  - announcing when the courses will start.
- Write **40–50** words on a separate sheet.

Memo

To:

From:

Date:

Subject:

PART TWO

- Your company exports to a number of countries around the world and is looking for a new agent for international freight. The Export Sales Manager has asked you to write a proposal saying which agent you recommend.
- Read the two advertisements below, on which you have already made some notes.
- Then, using **all** your handwritten notes, write your **proposal** for the Export Sales Manager.
- Write **120–140** words on a separate sheet.

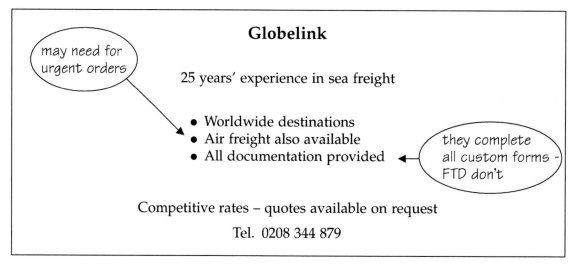

Globelink

25 years' experience in sea freight

- Worldwide destinations
- Air freight also available
- All documentation provided

may need for urgent orders

they complete all custom forms – FTD don't

Competitive rates – quotes available on request

Tel. 0208 344 879

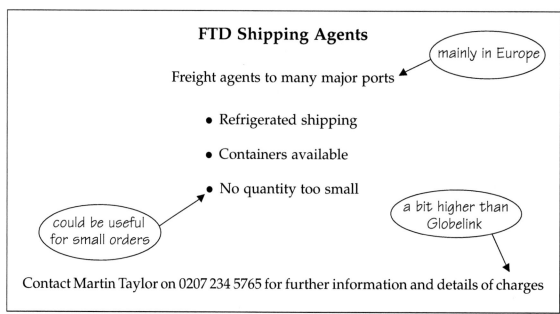

FTD Shipping Agents

Freight agents to many major ports

mainly in Europe

- Refrigerated shipping

- Containers available

- No quantity too small

could be useful for small orders

a bit higher than Globelink

Contact Martin Taylor on 0207 234 5765 for further information and details of charges

LISTENING   40 minutes (including 10 minutes' transfer time)

LISTENING

PART ONE

Questions 1–12

- You will hear three telephone conversations.
- Write **one or two words or a number** in the numbered spaces on the notes or forms.
- After you have listened once, replay the recording.

Conversation One (Questions 1–4)

- Look at the form below.
- You will hear a woman telephoning about some problems with an order.

Stationery Supplies International

CUSTOMER SERVICES / ORDER AMENDMENT FORM

Customer: Fenmore Consultants / Jennifer Gardiner

Order No: **(1)** ....

PROBLEMS

- paper: ordered A5 not A4

- envelopes: ordered **(2)** .... not white

- ink cartridges: ordered 20 Trujet **(3)** ....

COMMENTS

Correct items to be sent out tonight by **(4)** ....

Conversation Two (Questions 5–8)

- Look at the note below.
- You will hear a man leaving a message on an answering machine.

☎ **RT COMMUNICATIONS**

Message received for: Joel Frisk, (5) .... Department

From: John Castellani, Loboprint

He's booked you in for four nights at the (6) .... Hotel.

You'll be met at the airport by the (7) ....

Presentation planned for Wednesday morning. Dinner in the evening.

Please confirm by midday Monday if additional (8) .... at hotel required.

Conversation Three (Questions 9–12)

- Look at the note below.
- You will hear a man enquiring about training courses.

Contact Training

Telephone Message

Dave Smith called from (**9**) .... about training.

Can we provide a one-week course on (**10**) .... ?

Would also like one-to-one courses in (**11**) ....

Recommended by someone from (**12**) ....

PART TWO

Questions 13–22

Section One
(Questions 13–17)

- You will hear five short recordings.
- For each recording, decide what the speaker's job is.
- Write one letter (**A–H**) next to the number of the recording.
- Do not use any letter more than once.
- After you have listened once, replay each recording.

13 ....

14 ....

15 ....

16 ....

17 ....

A	Personnel Manager
B	Sales Manager
C	Legal Adviser
D	Financial Adviser
E	Conference Organiser
F	Research and Development Officer
G	Advertising Executive
H	Bank Manager

Section Two
(Questions 18–22)

- You will hear another five recordings. Each speaker is leaving a message on an answering machine.
- For each recording, decide what the main reason is for the phone call.
- Write one letter (**A–H**) next to the number of the recording.
- Do not use any letter more than once.
- After you have listened once, replay each recording.

18 ....

19 ....

20 ....

21 ....

22 ....

A	explaining a problem
B	asking for information
C	reminding someone about some work
D	explaining a procedure
E	paying a compliment
F	agreeing to a plan
G	making an apology
H	giving instructions

PART THREE

Questions 23–30

- You will hear an interview on local radio with Dr Tim Carter, the author of a book on how to give effective business presentations.
- For each question **23–30** mark one letter (**A**, **B** or **C**) for the correct answer.
- After you have listened once, replay the recording.

23 Dr Carter's book, *The Art of Giving Presentations*,

    A has come out recently.
    B was published last year.
    C will reach bookshops next year.

24 Dr Carter says he decided to improve his presentations because

    A he felt he was doing worse than his colleagues.
    B his boss expressed dissatisfaction with his performance.
    C he dislikes doing anything badly.

25 To improve his own performance Dr Carter studied

    A books about public speaking.
    B the techniques of good presenters.
    C common mistakes made by speakers.

26 What does Dr Carter say about nervousness?

    A There is no effective way to control it.
    B Audiences don't think it's a major problem.
    C He was given the wrong advice about it.

27 What was the first change Dr Carter made to his preparation?

    A He began practising alone in a big room.
    B He got colleagues to listen to his performance.
    C He began to develop key parts of his presentation.

28 Dr Carter now recommends making a video recording of

    A your practice presentation with colleagues present.
    B real presentations given by other people.
    C your practice presentation without an audience.

29 Dr Carter says most speakers find presentations hard because

    A they have to speak to unfriendly audiences.
    B they have little experience of public speaking.
    C they are anxious about the technical equipment.

30 What technique does Dr Carter recommend for reducing anxiety?

    A   relaxing the face muscles
    B   remembering a pleasant experience
    C   practising deep breathing

You now have 10 minutes to transfer your answers to your Answer Sheet.

SPEAKING 14 minutes

SAMPLE SPEAKING TASKS

PART 1

The interview – about 3 minutes
In this part the interlocutor asks questions to each of the candidates in turn. You have to give information about yourself and express personal opinions.

PART 2

'Mini presentation' – about 6 minutes
In this part of the test you are asked to give a short talk on a business topic. You have to choose one of the topics from the three below and then talk for about one minute. You have one minute to prepare your ideas.

A   WHAT IS IMPORTANT WHEN . . .?
CHOOSING SUITABLE TRANSPORT FOR
A BUSINESS TRIP

- CONVENIENCE
- COST-EFFECTIVENESS
-

B   WHAT IS IMPORTANT WHEN . . .?

SELECTING EMPLOYEES FOR PROMOTION

- PERSONAL QUALITIES
- CURRENT PERFORMANCE
-

C   WHAT IS IMPORTANT WHEN . . .?

SETTING UP A NEW BUSINESS

- MANAGEMENT EXPERIENCE
- FINANCIAL BACKING
-

PART 3

Discussion – about 5 minutes

In this part of the test you are given a discussion topic. You have 30 seconds to look at the prompt card, an example of which is below, and then about 3 minutes to discuss the topic with your partner. After that the examiner will ask you more questions related to the topic.

For **two** candidates

Company Visitors

A group of business people from a foreign trade delegation are visiting your company next month.
You have been asked to help prepare a programme of activities for the visitors.

Discuss the situation together, and decide:

- what kinds of activities would be suitable for the visitors
- how to entertain the visitors outside working hours

For **three** candidates

Company Visitors

A group of business people from a foreign trade delegation are visiting your company next month.
You have been asked to help prepare a programme of activities for the visitors.

Discuss the situation together, and decide:

- what kinds of activities would be suitable for the visitors
- which company personnel the visitors should meet
- how to entertain the visitors outside working hours

Test 2

READING   1 hour

PART ONE

Questions 1–7

- Look at the statements below and the details of conference centres on the opposite page.
- Which conference centre (**A, B, C** or **D**) does each statement **1–7** refer to?
- For each sentence **1–7**, mark one letter (**A, B, C,** or **D**) on your Answer Sheet.
- You will need to use some of the letters more than once.

Example:

0   There are various types of meeting rooms available here.

---

1 This conference centre is well known for the quality of its food.

2 Discounts are available for some clients.

3 There is someone on duty here at all times.

4 The very latest conference equipment is available here.

5 This conference centre now has a traditional atmosphere.

6 Secretarial support is available at no extra charge.

7 The centre is willing to give a refund if a client is not completely satisfied.

A

> **Sherwood House** is only a stone's throw away from the city centre and yet provides a stress-free and relaxing atmosphere for your business meetings. We have six meeting rooms, each with full conference facilities. Our reception desk is staffed round the clock, ready to deal with any calls; our highly experienced catering staff are responsible for an exciting variety of menus at affordable prices.

B

> **The Manor Hotel** is committed to giving you the perfect conference environment. As part of an extensive investment programme, all our meeting rooms have been upgraded to include the most up-to-date facilities. Our wide range of rooms will meet every possible need – one-to-one interviews, seminars, product lunches, major presentations etc. We also guarantee to return your fee should you be disappointed with our service.

C

> **Broomfield Hall**, a magnificent country house set in 80 acres of peaceful parkland, has been completely refurbished in order to re-create the elegance and comfort of times gone by. We have extensive conference facilities and specialist staff, dedicated to the success of your business event. We also offer special deals on accommodation for large delegations.

D

> **The Carlton Hotel**, conveniently situated just minutes from the motorway, is the ideal venue for your conference. Not only do we offer superb hospitality, but our fully equipped business centre provides a complete typing and copying service, included in the conference fee. The restaurant also enjoys an excellent reputation, offering everything from a midday sandwich to a formal dinner.

PART TWO

Questions 8–12

- Read the advice below about selling a business.
- Choose the best sentence from the opposite page to fill in each of the gaps.
- For each gap **8–12**, mark one letter (**A–G**) on your Answer Sheet.
- Do not use any letter more than once.
- There is an example at the beginning (**0**).

SELLING A BUSINESS

If you plan to sell your business, be careful. There are an enormous number of traps awaiting the inexperienced seller. Before giving out any information about the business to any potential purchaser, make sure they have signed a confidentiality undertaking – that is, a document promising not to make confidential information public. (**0**) ....*G*........ . Many confidentiality letters, however, have no legal value, so taking appropriate advice is recommended.

You should also consider your strategy for informing your staff of the proposed sale. Most business owners want to keep the sale secret from their employees until the deal has been completed – or at least until negotiations are fairly advanced. (**8**)................. . In addition, you will need to produce a considerable amount of information about the business and its running; for this you will require the co-operation of senior management, who will therefore need to be informed of the sale.

When corresponding with a potential purchaser mark everything 'Subject to Contract'. Contracts can be made accidentally and you do not want to be committed until a formal contract, including all of the relevant terms, has been negotiated and signed. To avoid this, many people negotiate a summary document which briefly sets out the main conditions of the sale. These documents can be useful because potential areas of dispute or disagreement can be seen in advance. (**9**)................. . Do remember, however, that a summary rarely deals with all the points for discussion which are going to arise in the course of negotiations.

Make sure all your paperwork is in order. (**10**)................. . It is vital therefore that you ensure all insurance policies, bank statements, finance documents, and employment, supplier and customer contracts are well ordered and up to date. This will save everyone a lot of time.

In addition, make sure that all staff have up-to-date contracts of employment. An employer must, by law, issue statements of terms of employment to all employees within two months of their starting work. (**11**)................. . Even if you fail to issue them the buyer will still expect you to be able to identify with certainty what the terms and conditions are. The absence of written contracts makes that much more difficult.

You may also need the approval of people entirely external to the business for the sale to take place. (**12**)................. . Getting such agreement generally takes time, so you will need to move quickly if a buyer wants it done before completing the deal.

Example: **0**

A These protect both the employer and the employee, and mean that there is certainty about those terms and conditions.

B This is the extent to which you can profit from the investment you have made in your business.

C A buyer will want to see vast quantities of information and documentation on the business.

D The most frequent example of this is when significant pieces of machinery and equipment are subject to financing arrangements, and the consent of the financier is necessary.

E They should be short and simple, and full agreement should be negotiated with the buyer as soon as possible.

F This can be difficult, though, and if staff find out about the sale it can unsettle them.

G You do not want a potential buyer using this confidential information either in the course of negotiations or after negotiations have broken down.

PART THREE

Questions 13–18

- Read the article below about business meetings and the questions on the opposite page.
- For each question **13–18**, mark one letter (**A**, **B**, **C** or **D**) on your Answer Sheet for the answer you choose.

GETTING THE MOST OUT OF MEETINGS

One aspect of business life which many managers are unhappy with is the need to attend meetings. Research indicates that managers will spend between a third and a half of their working lives in meetings. Although most managers would agree that it is hard to think of an alternative to meetings, as a means of considering information and making collective decisions, their length and frequency can cause problems with the workload of even the best-organised executives.

Meetings work best if they take place only when necessary and not as a matter of routine. One example of this is the discussion of personal or career matters between members of staff and their line and personnel managers. Another is during the early stages of a project when the team managing it need to learn to understand and trust one another.

Once it has been decided that a meeting is necessary, decisions need to be taken about who will attend and about the location and length of the meeting. People should only be invited to attend if they are directly involved in the matters under discussion and the agenda should be distributed well in advance. An agenda is vital because it acts as a road map to keep discussion focused and within the time limit allocated. This is also the responsibility of the person chairing the meeting, who should encourage those who say little to speak and stop those who have a great deal to say from talking too much.

At the end of a well organised meeting, people will feel that the meeting has been a success and be pleased they were invited. They will know not only what decisions were made but also the reasons for these decisions. Unfortunately, at the end of a badly organised meeting those present will leave feeling that they have wasted their time and that nothing worthwhile has been achieved.

Much thought has been given over the years to ways of keeping meetings short. One man who has no intention of spending half his working life in meetings is Roland Winterson, chief executive of a large manufacturing company. He believes that meetings should be short, sharp and infrequent. 'I try to hold no more than two or three meetings a week, attended by a maximum of three people for no longer than half an hour,' he says. 'They are clearly aimed at achieving a specific objective, such as making a decision or planning a strategy, and are based on careful preparation. I draw up the agenda for every meeting and circulate it in advance; those attending are expected to study it carefully and should be prepared to both ask and answer questions. Managers are best employed carrying out tasks directly connected with their jobs not attending endless meetings. In business, time is money and spending it in needless meetings that don't achieve anything can be very costly. Executives should follow the example of lawyers and put a cost on each hour of their time and then decide whether attending a long meeting really is the best way to spend their time.'

13 What do most managers think about meetings?

    A   Meetings take up most of their working life.
    B   Meetings allow them to monitor decision-making.
    C   Meetings prevent them from establishing a routine.
    D   Meetings are the only way they know of achieving certain objectives.

14 According to the writer, an example of a valuable meeting is one which

    A   allows colleagues to achieve a better working relationship
    B   requires managers to discuss staffing needs with personnel
    C   selects a suitable group of people to work together as a team
    D   encourages staff to present ideas on improvements in management

15 According to the writer the agenda is important because it

    A   is seen by everybody before the meeting.
    B   helps to give direction to the discussions.
    C   contains items of interest to all those present.
    D   shows who should speak at each stage of the meeting.

16 The writer says that people leaving a well organised meeting will understand

    A   the reason for their invitation to attend.
    B   how the decisions taken were relevant to them.
    C   the importance of proposals under discussion.
    D   why certain courses of action were agreed upon.

17 What does Roland Winterson say about the meetings that he organises?

    A   He aims to hold them on a regular basis.
    B   He ensures they have a definite purpose.
    C   He requires his managers to draw up the agenda.
    D   He uses them to make decisions about strategy.

18 What is Roland Winterson's opinion about meetings?

    A   They can be a bad use of a manager's time.
    B   Their importance is often underestimated.
    C   They frequently result in wrong decisions.
    D   Their effectiveness could be improved with better planning.

PART FOUR

Questions 19–33

- Read the text below about product brands.
- Choose the best word to fill each gap, from **A, B, C** or **D** on the opposite page.
- For each question **19–33**, mark one letter (**A, B, C** or **D**) on your Answer Sheet.
- There is an example at the beginning (**0**).

THE ROLE OF BRAND IMAGE

Although brand image is not the only (**0**) ......A...... why certain products are successful, it is an extremely important part of an overall marketing strategy. In fact, many manufacturers (**19**).................. such a high value on their brands that they employ legal experts to (**20**).................. them from misuse by imitators and counterfeit traders. In addition, companies (**21**).................. employees with handbooks which (**22**).................. how their logos should be used – for example the size and colour of graphics and suitable ways of displaying the product.

Originally the brand was little more than a graphic that helped people to (**23**).................. a particular product, but as advertising developed, it grew in (**24**).................. . As the famous brands became (**25**).................. with quality in the minds of consumers, manufacturers found they could (**26**).................. top prices for these products in order to recover some of the heavy (**27**).................. of advertising. As firms realised their potential value, brands quickly became registered trade marks. Today, branding is widespread and is used to sell both products and services.

Most companies (**28**).................. to achieve 'multiple appeal' with their brands. This means that the brand appeals to people of different age groups and lifestyles. The problem for the brand manufacturer is how to keep old customers and at the same time to (**29**).................. new ones.

A powerful brand is good for sales, but first this has to be (**30**).................. and then maintained through a continuous (**31**).................. of image design and advertising. If multiple appeal (**32**).................., then regular evaluation of the brand will show this and should (**33**).................. in the product being redesigned or the advertising being changed.

Example:

A reason   **B** factor   **C** influence   **D** cause

0	A	B	C	D
	▬	☐	☐	☐

19 **A** present   **B** place   **C** settle   **D** rest

20 **A** avoid   **B** control   **C** support   **D** protect

21 **A** provide   **B** give   **C** deliver   **D** arrange

22 **A** appoint   **B** specify   **C** assign   **D** prefer

23 **A** relate   **B** realise   **C** identify   **D** connect

24 **A** advantage   **B** concern   **C** benefit   **D** importance

25 **A** extended   **B** associated   **C** fixed   **D** attached

26 **A** charge   **B** instruct   **C** order   **D** bill

27 **A** payments   **B** costs   **C** amounts   **D** earnings

28 **A** pursue   **B** guide   **C** aim   **D** direct

29 **A** join   **B** earn   **C** bring   **D** attract

30 **A** thought   **B** created   **C** supposed   **D** caused

31 **A** method   **B** performance **C** attempt   **D** process

32 **A** fails   **B** defeats   **C** breaks   **D** loses

33 **A** produce   **B** lead   **C** result   **D** act

PART FIVE

Questions 34–45

- Read the text below about training.
- In most of the lines **34–45**, there is one extra word. It is either grammatically incorrect or does not fit in with the meaning of the text. Some lines, however, are correct.
- If a line is correct, write **CORRECT** on your Answer Sheet.
- If there is an extra word in the line, write **the extra word** in CAPITAL LETTERS on your Answer Sheet.

Examples:	0	T	H	A	T				
	00	C	O	R	R	E	C	T	

The cost of not training

0   Training is not a cost. It's an investment. It really doesn't matter that what we pay

00 for an investment. What is relevant is what we get in return. One of the easiest

34 ways is to put an organisation's future at risk would be to view training primarily as a

35 cost, and therefore provide with substandard training that operates only as a

36 temporary solution. Many companies attempt to quantify the results of training. For

37 example, a person paid $50,000 a year who wastes just one hour a day costs the

38 organisation between $6,250 per year. So if the organisation sends 25 people for

39 training and they all receive the same benefit, this would equal from $156,250

40 savings per year. A few years ago, training, apart from showing employees

41 what the basics of doing the job, was an optional extra for most organisations.

42 Today this is no longer the case. If we continue doing what we do in the same way,

43 most of us and our organisations will become obsolete within the five years. This is

44 because of our competitors are helping their staff to become more effective through

45 training. They understand that if the real price of not training is the company falling

behind as a result.

WRITING   45 minutes

WRITING

PART ONE

- You would like to go to a seminar on presentation skills.
- Write an **email** to your line manager:
  - requesting time off work to go to the seminar
  - saying when the seminar is
  - explaining why you want to go.
- Write **40–50** words on a separate sheet.

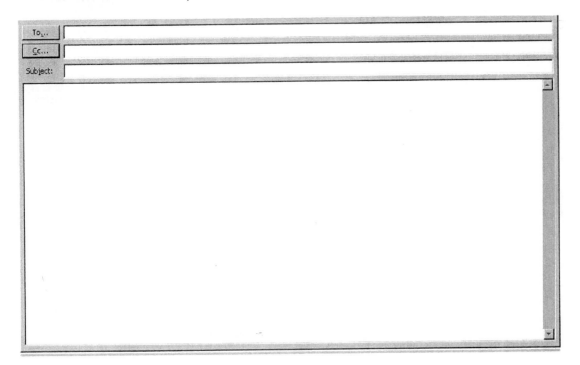

PART TWO

- You work for Bada, a retailer of sports goods. You have been asked to write a short report covering recent developments for store managers.
- Look at the graphs and email below, on which you have already made some handwritten notes.
- Then, using **all** your handwritten notes, write your **report** for store managers.
- Write **120–140** words on a separate sheet.

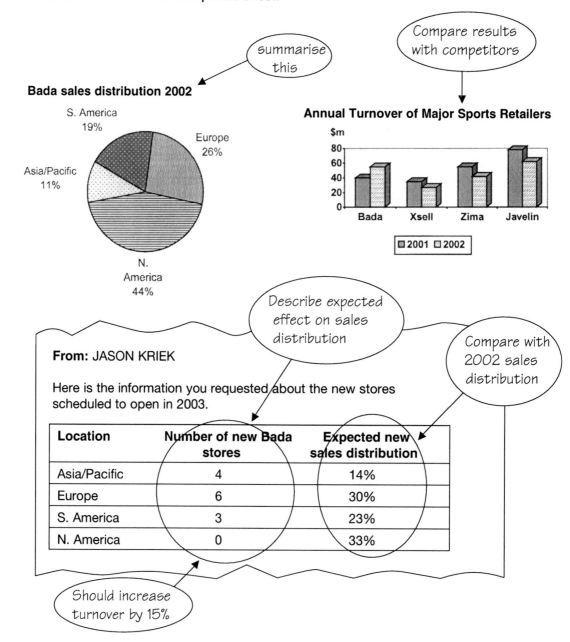

LISTENING   40 minutes (including 10 minutes' transfer time)

LISTENING

PART ONE

Questions 1–12

- You will hear three telephone conversations or messages.
- Write **one or two words or a number** in the numbered spaces on the notes or forms below.
- After you have listened once, replay each recording.

Conversation One (Questions 1–4)

- Look at the form below.
- You will hear a man making a request for catering.

**EXECUTIVE CATERING SERVICES
BOOKING FORM**

- -

Booking made by: Julian Russell

Company: Family Holidays

Event: Launch of new **(1)** ....

Date: **(2)** ....

Location: Head Office, in the **(3)** ....

Number attending: **(4)** ....

Conversation Two (Questions 5–8)

- Look at the note below.
- You will hear a man calling to change an arrangement.

Message

To: Sam Wong

From: Bob **(5)** .... (Planning Dept)

Message: Wednesday's meeting with him and **(6)** ....

              changed to **(7)** ...., at 11 am.

              Please bring **(8)** .... for the new production units.

Conversation Three (Questions 9–12)

- Look at the note below.
- You will hear two colleagues talking on the phone.

IT Department Messages   **Time:**   10.30am

Tom,

Dave Proctor **(9)** .... Dept) called - he has someone

who might be suitable for the **(10)** .... job.

Can you go over there and take a departmental **(11)** ....

with you?

Candidate will wait for up to **(12)** ....

PART TWO

Questions 13–22

Section One
(Questions 13–17)

- You will hear five short recordings.
- For each recording, decide what advice the speaker is giving.
- Write one letter (**A–H**) next to the number of the recording.
- Do not use any letter more than once.
- After you have listened once, replay each recording.

13 ....

14 ....

15 ....

16 ....

17 ....

A	begin and end the talk well
B	rehearse a few times beforehand
C	use clear visual materials
D	maximise eye contact with the audience
E	check all equipment thoroughly
F	look smart and business-like
G	avoid talking for too long
H	get the audience to participate

Section Two
(Questions 18–22)

- You will hear another five short recordings.
- Each speaker is talking on the phone.
- For each recording, decide the main reason for the phone call.
- Write one letter (**A–H**) next to the number of the recording.
- Do not use any letter more than once.
- After you have listened once, replay each recording.

18 ....

19 ....

20 ....

21 ....

22 ....

A	to ask for advice
B	to explain an error
C	to ask for a decision
D	to ask for information
E	to make a complaint
F	to request help
G	to confirm details
H	to express thanks

PART THREE

Questions 23–30

- You will hear an interview with Susan Gates, Director of Human Resources Policy at Robertson's, a national chain of supermarkets. She recently sat on a government committee that looked into the funding of higher education.
- For each question **23–30**, mark one letter (**A**, **B** or **C**) for the correct answer.
- After you have listened once, replay the recording.

23 Susan Gates thinks that the business community should have a role in higher education because

    A   business needs to compete with teaching as a graduate career choice.

    B   many courses are not vocational enough.

    C   many graduates enter the world of business.

24 Susan Gates thinks that the committee should include Robertson's because

    A   half of all graduates find jobs in retailing.

    B   the views of non-specialist employers need to be represented.

    C   it had more experience of employing graduates than IT companies.

25 Susan Gates says an important finding of the committee was that

    A   employers need graduates with skills in key areas.

    B   an increasing number of graduates had good IT skills.

    C   the demands of the workplace were unlikely to change.

26 What does Susan Gates say about numeracy?

    A   Top organisations train staff to work quickly with numbers.

    B   Most graduates are not confident with mathematics.

    C   Top employees are good with figures.

27 Susan Gates says that work experience for students

    A   enables them to decide what they want to do.

    B   provides industry with a flexible workforce.

    C   helps them to improve their job prospects.

28 What is Susan Gates' opinion of the research work carried out in higher education?

    A   It ought to benefit the economy more.

    B   It is a direct result of links with business.

    C   It has made British companies more competitive.

29 Susan Gates thinks that small businesses

    A   want graduates who need little training.

    B   cannot attract as many graduates as large organisations.

    C   need graduates with specialist skills.

30 Susan Gates says that the worlds of business and higher education should try to

    A   invest more money in research.

    B   share their expertise in more ways.

    C   improve the way they deal with change.

You now have 10 minutes to transfer your answers to your Answer Sheet.

SPEAKING   14 minutes

SAMPLE SPEAKING TASKS

PART 1

The interview – about 3 minutes
In this part the interlocutor asks questions to each of the candidates in turn. You
have to give information about yourself and express personal opinions.

PART 2

'Mini presentation' – about 6 minutes
In this part of the test you are asked to give a short talk on a business topic. You
have to choose one of the topics from the three below and then talk for about one
minute. You have one minute to prepare your ideas.

> **A   WHAT IS IMPORTANT WHEN . . .?**
>
> **DECIDING WHETHER TO APPLY FOR A NEW POST**
>
> - **LOCATION**
> - **CAREER PROSPECTS**
> -

> **B   WHAT IS IMPORTANT WHEN . . .?**
>
> **ORGANISING AN IN-HOUSE TRAINING COURSE**
>
> - **COURSE CONTENTS**
> - **PARTICIPANTS SELECTED**
> -

> **C   WHAT IS IMPORTANT WHEN . . .?**
>
> **RECRUITING SENIOR STAFF**
>
> - **RECRUITMENT AGENCIES**
> - **FINANCIAL INCENTIVES**
> -

PART 3

Discussion – about 5 minutes

In this part of the test you are given a discussion topic. You have 30 seconds to look at the prompt card, an example of which is below, and then about 3 minutes to discuss the topic with your partner. After that the examiner will ask you more questions related to the topic.

For **two** candidates

Customer Newsletter

Your company would like to introduce a newsletter to send to its customers regularly.
You have been asked to co-ordinate the project.

Discuss the situation together, and decide:

- what kinds of articles and information should be included in the newsletter
- what the newsletter should look like and how often it should be produced

---

For **three** candidates

Customer Newsletter

Your company would like to introduce a newsletter to send to its customers regularly.
You have been asked to co-ordinate the project.

Discuss the situation together, and decide:

- what kinds of articles and information should be included in the newsletter
- who should be asked to write for the newsletter
- what the newsletter should look like and how often it should be produced

---

Test 3

READING   1 hour

PART ONE

Questions 1–7

- Look at the statements below and the advertisements on the opposite page.
- Which advertisement does each statement **1–7** refer to?
- For each sentence **1–7**, mark one letter (**A, B, C,** or **D**) on your Answer Sheet.
- You will need to use some of the letters more than once.

Example:

0 You need to be familiar with a variety of computer software.

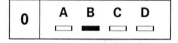

---

1 This job involves working for a well-known company.

2 You will meet a wide variety of customers in this job.

3 This post involves responsibility for recruitment.

4 Your work should not be discussed outside the office.

5 In this job you will deal with people's investments.

6 This post has recently been established.

7 Your job description will require you to read some documents very carefully.

A

> **ILT Consultants   £19,000 + benefits**
>
> Here's an exciting opportunity to combine your presentation skills and organisational abilities, working for a team of systems analysts. You will need to have a good eye for detail as the role involves large amounts of proof reading and checking. The job also involves client liaison at all levels, as well as an element of research.

B

> **John Guild & Son   £17,500 + benefits**
>
> City finance house seeks a mature person to work for the Secretariat. The post involves: looking after customers' financial assets such as property and possessions; database work; accounting; and organisational responsibilities. The bulk of the workload is highly confidential. A good level and range of PC experience will secure you an interview.

C

> **Hooper's   £17,000**
>
> Join this household name and play a key part in supporting their Regional Operations Director and Marketing team. This is a newly-created position within a well-established firm and there is plenty of opportunity for you to develop your role. You will need to be self-motivated with the ability to prioritise. Some Windows experience essential.

D

> **ITC Investment Consultants   £18,000 +**
>
> This is an opening for a bright, part-qualified assistant to work in an investment company's busy personnel department. You will need to have one year's experience of interviewing job applicants, and the confidence to handle appraisals and disciplinary actions. Further training will be offered for the right candidate. Keyboard skills are desirable as you will manage all personal correspondence.

PART TWO

Questions 8–12

- Read the article below which reviews a new book on company planning.
- Choose the best sentence from the list on the opposite page to fill each of the gaps.
- For each gap **8–12**, mark one letter (**A–G**) on your Answer Sheet.
- Do not use any letter more than once.
- There is an example at the beginning (**0**).

Firms need a better way of planning

Nick Field, in his book *Strategy Management,* **offers a new approach to help companies map out their future.**

Many companies have lost the art of strategy-making. They spend too much time looking at process change, organisation and systems. (**0**) ....*G*......... . They have got things out of balance. In many companies, the development of strategy is in crisis.

In a recent magazine poll, only six per cent of executives rated their company highly for long-term planning skills. (**8**).................. . If this figure is accurate, it is not surprising that 29% of the FTSE 100 companies failed to achieve real sales growth between 1992 and 1996, when take-overs are excluded from the figures.

There can be no doubt about the value of effective strategy-making. Recent research has shown that what are described as 'visionary' companies – those with clear strategies for the future – deliver higher shareholder returns. They are less at risk from short-term earnings pressures because they know – and they can convince others – that they will survive these.

(**9**)................. . Times have changed. The big company of today is not being defeated by another big company but by the small companies. So how do they do it? And where do companies that are failing in this respect turn? If a company accepts that their strategy development is not 'the best in the class', if they acknowledge that they need to do more to map out their future, influence rather than be influenced, shape their market instead of being shaped by it, how should they take on this strategy-making challenge?

Field's book *Strategy Management* puts forward a new approach to help companies rediscover the power of forward planning. (**10**).................. . The book is straightforward to understand and use, and offers practical and specific directions. Research and empirical testing have proved that it can be useful in all areas of industry and should be of value to any company.

The approach put forward is based on two key building blocks, the first being that any company considering its future must have a commitment to win. (**11**)................. . The second building block is competitive advantage. The author defines four prime areas that differentiate organisations and influence purchase decisions. These are 'the *performance* of the product or service, sold at the most attractive *price*, with extraordinary levels of *service* and strong *emotional values.*' It may require only one of these areas to produce a competitive advantage. Take Coca-Cola for example. (**12**).................. .

Companies can explore how to win by building on their commitment and working around this approach to identify which one or more of these four sources of advantage will lead to success.

Example:

A Clear guidelines are given on how to become involved with customers and build new forms of competitive advantage.

B Through the brand name, the company has established a relationship with customers' feelings that has made the product highly successful.

C Another survey estimated that only one in ten companies had the information they needed to make strategic decisions.

D Lacking any debate about the future, these are typically reduced to a once-a-year form-filling exercise.

E If this comes across forcefully enough rivals will see it and go elsewhere, believing the market will be taken over by another.

F In the past, it was generally believed that the scale of the company was the most significant factor.

G They do not invest enough effort in determining where they want to be in their markets and how they are going to beat their competitors.

PART THREE

Questions 13–18

- Read the article below about how to avoid working long hours and the questions on the opposite page.
- For each question **13–18**, mark one letter (**A**, **B**, **C** or **D**) on your Answer Sheet, for the answer you choose.

Morning, noon and night
The long-hours culture at work

Working an eight-hour day is a luxury for most professional people. Nowadays, the only way to guarantee an eight-hour working day is to have the kind of job where you clock on and off. Those professionals who have managed to limit their hours to what was, 20 years ago, the average do not wish to identify themselves. 'I can quite easily achieve my work within a normal day, but I don't like to draw attention to it,' says one sales manager. 'People looked at me when I left at 5 o'clock. Now, I put paperwork in my bag. People assume I'm doing extra hours at home.'

But more typical is Mark, who works as an account manager. He says, 'My contract says I work from 9 until 5 with extra hours as necessary. It sounds as if the extra hours are exceptional. In fact, my job would be enough not only for me, but also for someone else part-time. The idea of an eight-hour day makes me laugh!' He says he has thought about going freelance but realises that this doesn't guarantee better working hours.

Professor Cary Cooper, occupational psychologist at the University of Manchester, is the author of the annual *Quality of Working Life* survey. The most recent survey found that 77% of managers in Britain work more than their contracted hours, and that this is having a damaging effect on their health, relationships and productivity. Professor Cooper is critical of the long-hours culture. He says that while bosses believe long hours lead to greater efficiency, there is no evidence to support this. 'In fact, the evidence shows that long hours make you ill.'

There are, he says, steps that can be taken. One is to accept that the in-tray will never be empty. 'There are always things to do. You just have to make the rule that on certain days you go home early.' Prioritising work and doing essential tasks first helps, he says. He also thinks it's time to criticise bad employers and unreasonable terms of employment. 'By all means, show commitment where necessary but when expectations are too high, people have to begin saying openly that they have a life outside of work.'

Personal development coach Mo Shapiro agrees that communication is important. Staff need to talk to managers about the working practices within a company. Both parties should feel that the expectations are realistic and allow them to have responsibilities and interests outside work. She recognises, however, that in many organisations the response might well be, 'If you want more interests outside work, then find another job'.

She believes that senior staff have a duty to set an example. 'I recently worked for a firm of solicitors where the partners started at 7.30am. What kind of message is that to send to the staff?' She believes there is no shame in working sensible hours – in fact quite the reverse. 'Some people might be in at 7.30 but will be doing very little. You can work really hard from 9 to 5 and achieve the same. If you find it difficult to achieve an eight-hour day, there is, as a last resort, the old trick of leaving your jacket on your chair and your computer switched on, even after you have left the building.'

13 What does the writer say in the first paragraph about people who work an eight-hour day?

- **A** They are reluctant to admit to this.
- **B** They are disliked by their colleagues.
- **C** They are limited to certain professions.
- **D** They often catch up on work in the evenings.

14 What does Mark say about his work?

- **A** His main concern is job security.
- **B** Too much of his time at work is wasted.
- **C** The terms of his contract are misleading.
- **D** He objects to being given other people's work.

15 What does Cary Cooper say about recent trends in the workplace?

- **A** He believes that a long working day is counter-productive.
- **B** He has doubts about the results of the *Quality of Working Life* survey.
- **C** He says that employers should accept the link between working hours and safety.
- **D** He argues that further research is needed into the relationship between work and health.

16 How does Cary Cooper think people should deal with the requirements of the workplace?

- **A** Obtain help in negotiating terms of employment.
- **B** Let people know when demands are unreasonable.
- **C** Delegate the less important work to other staff.
- **D** Accept that the modern workplace is a competitive place.

17 What does Mo Shapiro see as a problem for employees today?

- **A** They lack the communication skills that modern business requires.
- **B** Many employers would not regard requests for shorter hours favourably.
- **C** Most employers do not want to be responsible for the professional development of staff.
- **D** They have difficulties adapting to the rapid changes occurring in working practices.

18 What does Mo Shapiro think about present working hours?

- **A** In many companies senior staff need to work a long day.
- **B** The best staff are efficient enough to finish their work within eight hours.
- **C** There are too many staff deceiving employers about their hours of work.
- **D** Top executives should use their influence to change the long-hours culture.

PART FOUR

Questions 19–33

- Read the advice below on writing a CV.
- Choose the best word to fill each gap, from **A, B, C** or **D** on the opposite page.
- For each question **19–33**, mark one letter (**A, B, C** or **D**) on your Answer Sheet.
- There is an example at the beginning (**0**).

Guidelines for Writing Your CV
A well-produced CV can make all the difference when applying for a job.

It can take a reader just 30 seconds to (**0**) ......B...... a decision about a CV. So when writing a CV, you should remember you have just half a minute to (**19**).................. the reader's interest, leave a clear (**20**).................. of professionalism and indicate the likely (**21**).................. to an employer of hiring you. To prepare a CV which is (**22**).................. will take time and possibly several drafts. Layout, presentation and a choice of words which demonstrate both responsibility and achievement are vital (**23**).................. of any CV.

No matter how well your career background and skills (**24**).................. the needs of an employer, your efforts could (**25**).................. if you make it difficult for the reader to take in the relevant information. As your message must register quickly, make the reader's task an easy one. (**26**).................. that the print is well spaced and that the key information is displayed clearly.

The (**27**).................. of the CV is to generate interviews. Visually, you want your CV to have a positive effect, but it is also necessary for it to (**28**).................. the reader that you are worth meeting. The style in which you present your CV is a (**29**).................. of personal choice, but it is important that you use words which (**30**).................. an active and successful career.

People sometimes make the mistake of (**31**).................. a CV as a rewrite of their job description, which results in unnecessary jargon and detail. In addition, issues such as salary and (**32**).................. for leaving previous employers should not be (**33**)..................; they are best discussed at the first interview stage.

Example:

A meet   **B** reach   **C** arrive   **D** contact

0	A	B	C	D
	▢	▬	▢	▢

19	**A** take	**B** realise	**C** gain	**D** collect
20	**A** influence	**B** impression	**C** meaning	**D** symbol
21	**A** resource	**B** credit	**C** benefit	**D** asset
22	**A** certain	**B** efficient	**C** capable	**D** effective
23	**A** components	**B** sections	**C** pieces	**D** sectors
24	**A** correspond	**B** match	**C** coordinate	**D** agree
25	**A** decline	**B** fold	**C** collapse	**D** fail
26	**A** Ensure	**B** Allow	**C** Confirm	**D** Guarantee
27	**A** incentive	**B** purpose	**C** result	**D** motive
28	**A** decide	**B** prompt	**C** convince	**D** determine
29	**A** subject	**B** condition	**C** situation	**D** matter
30	**A** inform	**B** suggest	**C** appear	**D** instruct
31	**A** calculating	**B** supposing	**C** estimating	**D** regarding
32	**A** reasons	**B** intentions	**C** opinions	**D** conclusions
33	**A** held	**B** contained	**C** included	**D** concerned

PART FIVE

Questions 34–45

- Read the text below about customer loyalty.
- In most of the lines **34–45**, there is one extra word. It is either grammatically incorrect or does not fit in with the sense of the text. Some lines, however, are correct.
- If a line is correct, write **CORRECT** on your Answer Sheet.
- If there is an extra word in the line, write **the extra word** in CAPITAL LETTERS on your Answer Sheet.

Examples:	0	C	O	R	R	E	C	T	
	00	I	T						

Increasing Customer Loyalty

0 Customers are not revolutionaries. They are attracted to the certainty of knowing that

00 what they buy it will be good value for money or will perform a particular task effectively.

34 They are cautious but their loyalty, without once achieved, is the key to business success.

35 Brands can help to create customer loyalty by providing us a signpost to certainty and

36 safety. Ideally, when a customer sees a product, it leads to a range of positive thoughts

37 so that the product is bought. Unfortunately, only a small number of products have

38 reached to this level. While everyone in business is aware of the need to attract and

39 retain customers, that they often overlook the second, more important, half of the

40 equation. In the excitement of beating against the competition and securing orders,

41 managers often fail to ensure that the customer remains a customer. It has been

42 estimated that since the average company loses between 10 and 30% of its customers

43 every year and this only recently have organisations started to wake up to these lost

44 opportunities and to calculate the financial implications. Established customers often buy

45 lot more and, and in addition, they may also provide free word-of-mouth advertising.

WRITING   45 minutes

WRITING

PART ONE

- You are a manager in a company which manufactures office furniture. Next month you are going to London to discuss an important contract.
- Write a **note** to your assistant:
  - saying when you want to leave and return
  - asking him to book flights
  - telling him which hotel to book.
- Write **40–50** words on a separate sheet.

PART TWO

- You recently attended a one-day training course on health and safety. You were disappointed with the course and you have decided to write a letter of complaint to the training company.
- Read the advertisement below, which gives details of the course. You have already made some notes on the advertisement.
- Then, using **all** your handwritten notes, write your **letter** to Moira Geddings at GBG Certification Services.
- Do not include postal addresses.
- Write **120–140** words a separate sheet.

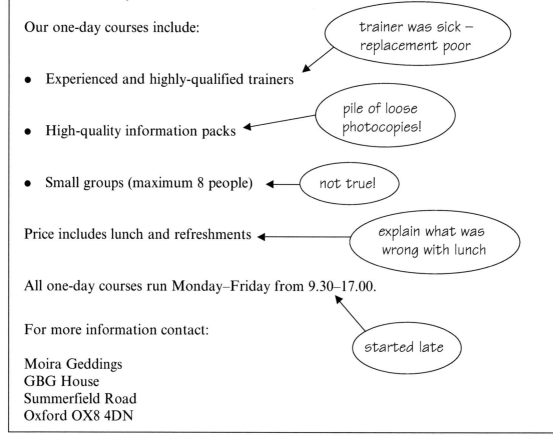

GBG Certification Services
Good for business, good for you.

Regardless of whether you are in a manufacturing or service industry, you are required by law to operate your business in a manner which is safe and healthy for your workforce. Our courses will help you provide a safe and legally sound working environment for your staff.

Our one-day courses include:

- Experienced and highly-qualified trainers

  trainer was sick – replacement poor

- High-quality information packs

  pile of loose photocopies!

- Small groups (maximum 8 people)

  not true!

Price includes lunch and refreshments

  explain what was wrong with lunch

All one-day courses run Monday–Friday from 9.30–17.00.

  started late

For more information contact:

Moira Geddings
GBG House
Summerfield Road
Oxford OX8 4DN

LISTENING   40 minutes (including 10 minutes' transfer time)

LISTENING

PART ONE

Questions 1–12

- You will hear three telephone conversations or messages.
- Write **one or two words or a number** in the numbered spaces on the notes or forms below.
- After you have listened once, replay each recording.

Conversation One (Questions 1–4)

- Look at the note below.
- You will hear a man making a call about a delivery.

Telephone Message

To: John White

Date: 19/10/00

Patrick Fisher rang to say our new **(1)** .... would be

delivered tomorrow. You need to tell Sarah Robbins, the **(2)** .... ,

where to **(3)** .... them.

Please phone Mr Fisher on **(4)** .... if there are any

problems.

Conversation Two (Questions 5–8)

- Look at the note below.
- You will hear a man telephoning his personnel officer.

Message

Date: 12 November 00

From: Roshan Singh, **(5)** .... Department.

Message: He has received an interesting **(6)** ....

and wants to discuss **(7)** ....

He has to reply by **(8)** ....

Conversation Three (Questions 9–12)

● Look at the note below.
● You will hear a woman calling a company about a possible order.

TELEPHONE ENQUIRY RECORD

Caller: Julie Ventnor from Polareach Ltd

She's interested in our **(9)** ....

Requires details of our **(10)** ....

Total monthly order: approx. **(11)** £ ....

Meeting on: **(12)** ....

PART TWO

Questions 13–22

Section One
(Questions 13–17)

- You will hear five short recordings. Each speaker is saying what a manager must do to achieve success.
- For each recording, decide which is the most important action for that speaker.
- Write one letter (**A–H**) next to the number of the recording.
- Do not use any letter more than once.
- After you have listened once, replay each recording.

13 ....

14 ....

15 ....

16 ....

17 ....

A	sort out staff disagreements
B	delegate tasks fairly
C	obtain all the facts
D	develop a range of strategies
E	establish clear goals
F	carry out regular planning
G	clarify all job descriptions
H	act immediately

Section Two
(Questions 18–22)

- You will hear another five short recordings. Each speaker is talking about a visitor to the office.
- For each recording, decide which visitor the speaker is talking about.
- Write one letter (**A–H**) next to the number of the recording.
- Do not use any letter more than once.
- After you have listened once, replay each recording.

18 ....

19 ....

20 ....

21 ....

22 ....

A	a health and safety official
B	an estate agent
C	an insurance broker
D	a journalist
E	a foreign buyer
F	a lawyer
G	a marketing consultant
H	a travel agent

PART THREE

Questions 23–30

- You will hear a radio interview with Richard Wood, the founder of Bookstore, a company that sells books on the internet.
- For each question **23–30** mark one letter (**A, B** or **C**) for the correct answer.
- After you have listened once, replay the recording.

23 Richard Wood started the internet company, Bookstore, because he felt

   A he was earning very little in his job.
   B he had reached the age for a career change.
   C he had to respond to a business opportunity.

24 What did Richard Wood consider when choosing his product?

   A whether the suppliers could respond quickly to demand
   B whether customers would be worried about the price
   C whether the product could be distributed around the world easily

25 Why did Richard Wood decide on books and not CDs as his product?

   A The demand for books is more international.
   B People with computers buy many books.
   C There is a greater range of book titles available.

26 According to Richard Wood, what has been an important element in Bookstore's success?

   A attracting good personnel
   B the many new ideas that were generated
   C his knowledge of computer software

27 What was Bookstore's sales revenue at the end of 1997?

   A $120 million
   B $230 million
   C $310 million

28 Bookstore's profits are low because of

   A money spent on promotion.
   B fluctuations in the stock market.
   C changes in the management structure.

29 Why is Bookstore's customer service so successful?

    A   The company is able to offer any book title in print.

    B   The company deals with complaints in a positive way.

    C   The company gives priority to orders from regular customers.

30 Bookstore can perform better than its competitors because

    A   its distribution network is more efficient.

    B   it has a wider share of the international market.

    C   its staff have a personal investment in the company.

You now have 10 minutes to transfer your answers to your Answer Sheet.

SPEAKING   14 minutes

SAMPLE SPEAKING TASKS

PART 1

The interview – about 3 minutes
In this part the interlocutor asks questions to each of the candidates in turn. You have to give information about yourself and express personal opinions.

PART 2

'Mini presentation' – about 6 minutes
In this part of the test you are asked to give a short talk on a business topic. You have to choose one of the topics from the three below and then talk for about one minute. You have one minute to prepare your ideas.

A   WHAT IS IMPORTANT WHEN . . .?

ATTENDING AN INTERVIEW

- **APPEARANCE OF APPLICANT**
- **APPLICANT'S KNOWLEDGE OF COMPANY**
-

B   WHAT IS IMPORTANT WHEN . . .?

PLANNING MARKET RESEARCH

- **TYPES OF QUESTIONS**
- **TYPE OF PEOPLE**
-

C   WHAT IS IMPORTANT WHEN . . .?

PREDICTING PROFITS

- **CURRENT SALES FIGURES**
- **MARKET TRENDS**
-

PART 3

Discussion – about 5 minutes

In this part of the test you are given a discussion topic. You have 30 seconds to look at the prompt card, an example of which is below, and then about 3 minutes to discuss the topic with your partner. After that the examiner will ask you more questions related to the topic.

For **two** candidates

Promotion Video

Your company is planning to produce a short video to promote itself abroad. You have been asked to help plan the contents of the video.

Discuss the situation together, and decide:

- who the target audience will be, and how to make the video interesting and informative for them
- which aspects of the company you will need to include on the video

For **three** candidates

Promotion Video

Your company is planning to produce a short video to promote itself abroad. You have been asked to help plan the contents of the video.

Discuss the situation together, and decide:

- who the target audience will be, and how to make the video interesting and informative for them
- which aspects of the company you will need to include on the video
- which employees should appear on the video and how to encourage them to participate

Test 4

READING 1 hour

READING

PART ONE

Questions 1–7

- Look at the statements below and the information about business schools on the opposite page.
- Which school (**A**, **B**, **C** and **D**) does each statement **1–7** refer to?
- For each sentence **1–7**, mark one letter (**A**, **B**, **C**, or **D**) on your Answer Sheet.
- You will need to use some of the letters more than once.

Example:

0 It has students of many different nationalities.

---

1 It can offer courses that are designed for the needs of specific companies.

2 It has been brought up to date by its new management.

3 Many students choose it because its contacts with industry may help them get work.

4 It is in a good location for attracting suitable staff.

5 Many of its students have gained influential positions in the business world.

6 Its premises have recently been expanded.

7 It has highly respected international staff.

A

LDA School of Management

LDA has the advantage of being within a few hours' drive of the hi-tech industries of Silicon Valley, which enables senior personnel from hi-tech companies to teach there. The school has prospered in recent years and offers its students excellent facilities. It attracts students from all over the world and has a fairly large intake of 30,000 students a year.

B

Dalchester School of Business

Under the leadership of Jon Richards, Dalchester has long been one of the world's top business schools. It is notably strong on its tailor-made executive programmes, which are written to meet each company's particular requirements. The Sinclair Centre, with new lecture rooms and a computer centre, has just been added to the school.

C

Radbridge School of Management

The reputation of the long-established RSM has been strengthened in recent years. This is mainly due to the appointment of Director Kim Taylor, who, with his programme of modernisation, has led the school into the age of Information Technology. Its network of former students remains second to none, with many having top positions in the world of finance and industry.

D

IBA Management School

This Swiss-based school has built its reputation on the quality and extent of its links with manufacturing and financial institutions. Its lecturers, who have been recruited from many different countries, are extremely well thought of in the business world. Student numbers average 25,000 a year. Many select the school because its links with industry are thought to help with employment prospects.

PART TWO

Questions 8–12

- Read the article below about telecommunications.
- Choose the best sentence from the opposite page to fill each of the gaps.
- For each gap **8–12**, mark one letter (**A–G**) on your Answer Sheet.
- Do not use any letter more than once.
- There is an example at the beginning (**0**).

THE CUSTOMER MAY NOT RING TWICE

Companies spend large sums of money on their telephone systems, but then use them to create the wrong image, according to Ben Lambert, International Performance Manager at a company called Octopus. (**0**) ....*G*........ . Some can take as long as 24 seconds to answer the phone. 'At one time you had to dial the number and wait for the exchange or an operator to connect you. You were aware that it was probably going to take time and if no-one picked up the phone you would probably hang on for 20 rings,' he says. 'Now you bang in the numbers and the phone rings at the other end almost before you have finished. (**8**).................. . Unless it is vital to get through, you are rarely prepared to wait as long as 24 seconds. In fact, the average response time should be five to ten seconds.'

Telephonists are one of the main interfaces with the public and customers. They give the first impression of the company and by definition you get only one chance to make a first impression. The facilities manager should know the fastest response time to the telephone, the slowest response time and the average response time. Mr Lambert points to a television advertisement by a leading bank that promised an answer within four rings. (**9**).................. . 'Banks are trying to promote themselves as service providers and this advertisement gave a very powerful message,' says Mr Lambert.

Octopus estimates that telecommunications is the most expensive support service in offices, costing on average £1,000 per employee each year. (**10**).................. . Given the changes over the past ten years, the cost of communicating is likely to continue to rise. In 1986, the typical office worker had just a simple push-button, or even dialling, handset. Now the traditional desk-based telephone also has voice mail and direct dialling and the staff member relies increasingly on email, paging, video-conferencing, on-line business services and mobile phones. Mr Lambert says, 'Such is the importance of all this to regions and economies generally that cities are increasingly looking on communications as the key infrastructure issue. (**11**).................. . They are becoming as important, if not more so, than physical communications.'

Telephony can sometimes get too sophisticated, though. Some American companies, for example, are refusing to install automatic answering systems that tell callers to dial extension numbers. (**12**).................. . This gives the opposite impression to the one that companies would like to project.

Example:

A This was a very simple strategy that created a new performance measure.

B Considering the cost of facilities, better systems are out of the question.

C You expect an equally quick response.

D Atlanta, for example, used the Olympic games as an opportunity to become one of the best places in the world for multimedia communications.

E In many cases these are left on all day and the caller is passed automatically from one office to another.

F It is second only to wages within the average company budget.

G He claims that many companies have an average response time of 17 seconds for incoming calls.

PART THREE

Questions 13–18

- Read the article below about managing a small business and the questions on the opposite page.
- For each question **13–18**, mark one letter (**A**, **B**, **C** or **D**) on your Answer Sheet, for the answer you choose.

The Difficulties Of Managing A Small Business

Ronald Meers asks who chief executives of entrepreneurial or small businesses can turn to for advice.

'The organisational weaknesses that entrepreneurs have to deal with every day would cause the managers of a mature company to panic,' Andrew Bidden wrote recently in *Boston Business Review*. This seems to suggest that the leaders of entrepreneurial or small businesses must be unlike other managers, or the problems faced by such leaders must be the subject of a specialised body of wisdom, or possibly both. Unfortunately, neither is true. Not much worth reading about managing the entrepreneurial or small business has been written, and the leaders of such businesses are made of flesh and blood, like the rest of us.

Furthermore, little has been done to address the aspects of entrepreneurial or small businesses that are so difficult to deal with and so different from the challenges faced by management in big business. In part this is because those involved in gathering expertise about business and in selling advice to businesses have historically been more interested in the needs of big business. In part, in the UK at least, it is also because small businesses have always preferred to adapt to changing circumstances.

The organisational problems of entrepreneurial or small businesses are thus forced upon the individuals who lead them. Even more so than for bigger businesses, the old saying is true – that people, particularly those who make the important decisions, are a business's most important asset. The research that does exist shows that neither money nor the ability to access more of it is the major factor determining growth. The main reason an entrepreneurial business stops growing is the lack of management and leadership resource available to the business when it matters. Give an entrepreneur an experienced, skilled team and he or she will find the funds every time. Getting the team, though, is the difficult bit.

Part of the problem for entrepreneurs is the speed of change that affects their businesses. They have to cope with continuous change yet have always been suspicious about the latest 'management solution'. They regard the many offerings from business schools as out of date even before they leave the planning board and have little faith in the recommendations of consultants when they arrive in the hands of young, inexperienced graduates. But such impatience with 'management solutions' does not mean that problems can be left to solve themselves. However, the leaders of growing businesses are still left with the problem of who to turn to for advice.

The answer is horribly simple: leaders of small businesses can ask each other. The collective knowledge of a group of leaders can prove enormously helpful in solving the specific problems of individuals. One leader's problems have certainly been solved already by someone else. There is an organisation called KITE which enables those responsible for small businesses to meet. Its members, all of whom are chief executives, go through a demanding selection process, and then join a small group of other chief executives. They come from a range of business sectors and each offers a different corporate history. Each group is led by a 'moderator', an independently selected businessman or woman who has been specially trained to head the group. Each member takes it in turn to host a meeting at his or her business premises and, most important of all, group discussions are kept strictly confidential. This encourages a free sharing of problems and increases the possibility of solutions being discovered.

13 What does the writer say about entrepreneurs in the first paragraph?

    A   It is wrong to assume that they are different from other managers.

    B   The problems they have to cope with are specific to small businesses.

    C   They find it difficult to attract staff with sufficient expertise.

    D   They could learn from the organisational skills of managers in large companies.

14 According to the second paragraph, what has led to a lack of support for entrepreneurs?

    A   Entrepreneurs have always preferred to act independently.

    B   The requirements of big businesses have always taken priority.

    C   It is difficult to find solutions to the problems faced by entrepreneurs.

    D   Entrepreneurs are reluctant to provide information about their businesses.

15 What does the writer say about the expansion of small businesses?

    A   Many small businesses do not produce enough profits to finance growth.

    B   Many employees in small businesses have problems working as part of a team.

    C   Being able to recruit the right people is the most important factor affecting growth.

    D   Leaders of small businesses lack the experience to make their companies a success.

16 What does the writer say is an additional problem for entrepreneurs in the fourth paragraph?

    A   They rely on management systems that are out of date.

    B   They will not adopt measures that provide long-term solutions.

    C   They have little confidence in the business advice that is available.

    D   They do not take market changes into account when drawing up business plans.

17 What does the writer say the members of the KITE organisation provide?

    A   Advice on how to select suitable staff.

    B   A means of contacting potential clients.

    C   A simple checklist for analysing problems.

    D   Direct experience of a number of industries.

18 The writer says that KITE groups are likely to succeed because

    A   members are able to elect their leader.

    B   the leaders have received extensive training.

    C   members are encouraged to adopt a critical approach.

    D   information is not passed on to non-members.

PART FOUR

Questions 19–33

- Read the text below about the start of a new business.
- Choose the best word to fill each gap, from **A**, **B**, **C** or **D** on the opposite page.
- For each question **19–33**, mark one letter (**A**, **B**, **C** or **D**) on your Answer Sheet.
- There is an example at the beginning (**0**).

In 1998, 25-year old John Stewart was (**0**) ......B...... redundant. He was left with a compensation (**19**)................. of £5,000 and a determination to be his own (**20**)................. . As a supporter of his local football club, he had often helped them by maintaining and repairing their seating. He now (**21**)................. to set up his own company and make a (**22**)................. out of his hobby.

His first (**23**)................. was to get 1,000 brochures printed, (**24**)................. the two main services which he could (**25**)................., repair and maintenance. He sent these brochures to amateur and professional football clubs, and other similar (**26**)................., such as hockey clubs.

The week after completing the mailing was the worst of his life. He had no responses at all. Then a letter arrived from Scotland inviting him to give a (**27**)................. for a pre-season check of a football club's seating. He arrived in Scotland in three hours; by the end of the afternoon he had signed the (**28**)................. to do the work. For £500 the club had its seating made good, and on arriving home three days later, John worked (**29**)................. that he had made a £250 (**30**)................. .

The next four weeks were extremely busy, as club after club (**31**)................. John to work for them. He priced each job in the same way as the first, working out all the direct (**32**)................., then adding 100%. Money started to flow in and John bought a van and rented a factory unit on an industrial estate near his house.

Then in late August the phones stopped (**33**)................. as the pre-season work dried up. John realised that he needed longer-term work and decided to move into the manufacture of seating for new sports stadiums and the replacement market.

Example:

A told   **B** made   **C** required   **D** found

0	**A**	**B**	**C**	**D**
	☐	☐	☐	▬

19 **A** salary   **B** wage   **C** payment   **D** amount

20 **A** boss   **B** worker   **C** businessman   **D** head

21 **A** accepted   **B** thought   **C** liked   **D** decided

22 **A** living   **B** practice   **C** labour   **D** task

23 **A** stage   **B** point   **C** movement   **D** step

24 **A** declaring   **B** expressing   **C** outlining   **D** designing

25 **A** do   **B** provide   **C** achieve   **D** succeed

26 **A** organisations   **B** situations   **C** activities   **D** sports

27 **A** bid   **B** tender   **C** valuation   **D** quotation

28 **A** charge   **B** terms   **C** invoice   **D** contract

29 **A** out   **B** up   **C** off   **D** over

30 **A** profit   **B** credit   **C** receipt   **D** reward

31 **A** agreed   **B** invited   **C** ordered   **D** offered

32 **A** figures   **B** bills   **C** costs   **D** prices

33 **A** sounding   **B** answering   **C** ringing   **D** calling

PART FIVE

Questions 34–45

- Read the text below about delegating.
- In most of the lines **34–45**, there is one extra word. It is either grammatically incorrect or does not fit in with the sense of the text. Some lines, however, are correct.
- If a line is correct, write **CORRECT** on your Answer Sheet.
- If there is an extra word in the line, write **the extra word** in CAPITAL LETTERS on your Answer Sheet.

Examples:	0	C	O	R	R	E	C	T	
	00	T	H	E	Y				

THE ART OF DELEGATION

0   Are you one of those people who doesn't trust anyone else to do what needs to be

00 done? Some managers they can't bear anyone else to help them in any way. They

34 don't believe that anyone can do such a job as well as they can. It is not surprising

35 that they then get overwhelmed by work and complain that they have far too much

36 to do, but it could be argued that it is by their own fault. If they learnt to delegate,

37 they would have much more time available. Besides the saving time and freeing

38 them to concentrate on tasks that are important, delegating also benefits to the

39 company. If managers delegate effectively, their staff will become more skilled and

40 committed. Asking staff to take those decisions improves their efficiency and

41 morale. This will contribute it not only to the success of the team, but to the success

42 of the company as a whole. More importantly, it will also show how good that a

43 person's managerial skills are, which is useful when candidates are considered for

44 promotion. Trusting other people to do a job properly and in providing them with the

45 opportunity to do so is therefore an essential management skill in all the workplace

of today.

WRITING 45 minutes

WRITING

PART ONE

- Your company's Sales Department has asked you to give a talk next Friday on your most recent project.
- Write an **email** to Mrs Jay in the Sales Department:
  - agreeing to give the talk and suggesting a time
  - saying what equipment you will need
  - requesting information about the participants.
- Write **40–50** words on a separate sheet.

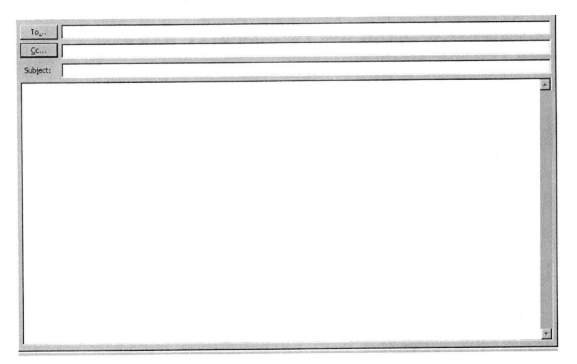

PART TWO

- The company you work for is expanding rapidly and is looking for new premises. Your Managing Director is interested in Waterside Industrial Park, and has asked you to write a letter to find out more information.
- Read Waterside Industrial Park's advertisement below, on which your Managing Director has already made some notes.
- Then, using **all** your Managing Director's handwritten notes, write your **letter** to Rosemary Brown at Waterside Industrial Park.
- Do not include postal addresses.
- Write **120–140** words on a separate sheet.

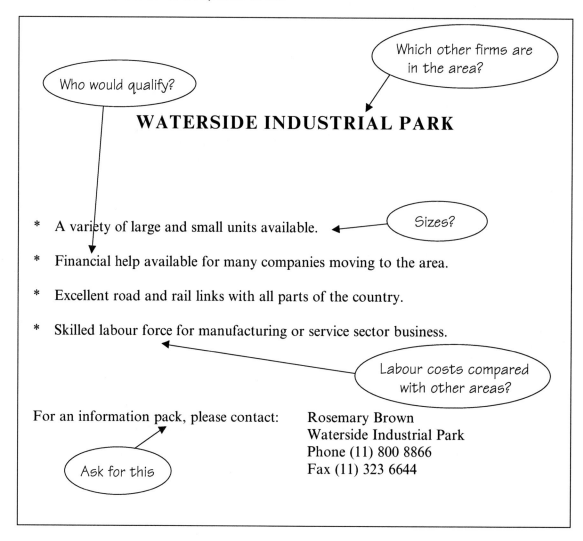

Which other firms are in the area?

Who would qualify?

WATERSIDE INDUSTRIAL PARK

Sizes?

* A variety of large and small units available.

* Financial help available for many companies moving to the area.

* Excellent road and rail links with all parts of the country.

* Skilled labour force for manufacturing or service sector business.

Labour costs compared with other areas?

For an information pack, please contact:

Ask for this

Rosemary Brown
Waterside Industrial Park
Phone (11) 800 8866
Fax (11) 323 6644

LISTENING   40 minutes (including 10 minutes' transfer time)

LISTENING

PART ONE

Questions 1–12

- You will hear three telephone conversations or messages.
- Write **one or two words or a number** in the numbered spaces on the notes or forms below.
- After you have listened once, replay each recording.

Conversation One (Questions 1–4)

- Look at the notes below.
- You will hear a man phoning for a job application.

CJ PRODUCTIONS
CJ Personnel
CJ Job Application Requests

Job: **(1)** .... (Marketing Department)

Reference Number: **(2)** ....

Advertised in: **(3)** ....

Name: Daniel Johnson

Address: Internal, c/o **(4)** ....

Conversation Two (Questions 5–8)

- Look at the notes below.
- You will hear a man telephoning a bank about a problem with an account.

HPR BANK
CUSTOMER SERVICES DIVISION

CUSTOMER: George Bliss, **(5)** .... of

Arundel Holdings

ACCOUNT NUMBER: **(6)** ....

PROBLEM: No record in his office of a **(7)** .... of

£15,000 on June 10th.

Also, can't be one of their **(8)** ....

- they all begin with 50. Want us to investigate.

Conversation Three (Questions 9–12)

- Look at the note below.
- You will hear a woman calling about a conference booking.

Message

To: Rachel Bould

Janet Shibuya (Conference Reservation Service) called about

(9) .... Seminar, 24th April.

Has made booking at the (10) .... Hotel.

Do we want the (11) .... - it's cheaper.

Send list of (12) .... needed by Friday.

PART TWO

Questions 13–22

Section One
(Questions 13–17)

- You will hear five short recordings. The five speakers are explaining what their jobs involve.
- For each recording, decide what the speaker's job is.
- Write one letter (**A–H**) next to the number of the recording.
- Do not use any letter more than once.
- After you have listened once, replay each recording.

13 ....

14 ....

15 ....

16 ....

17 ....

A	Finance Manager
B	Payroll Officer
C	Customer Services Manager
D	IT Systems Manager
E	Office Manager
F	Personnel Manager
G	Production Supervisor
H	Sales Representative

Section Two
(Questions 18–22)

- You will hear another five short recordings. Each speaker is describing a problem within a company.
- For each recording, decide in which area there is a problem.
- Write one letter (**A–H**) next to the number of the recording.
- Do not use any letter more than once.
- After you have listened once, replay each recording.

18 ....

19 ....

20 ....

21 ....

22 ....

A	after-sales service
B	company structure
C	internal communications
D	public relations
E	quality control
F	sales targets
G	staff absences
H	turnover of staff

PART THREE

Questions 23–30

- You will hear a radio interview with the Managing Director of a restaurant chain.
- For each question **23–30** mark one letter (**A**, **B** or **C**) for the correct answer.
- After you have listened once, replay the recording.

23 Olivia says that as a teenager she

    A   was taught at home.
    B   was very competitive.
    C   spent little time in one place.

24 What does Olivia say about her studies at university?

    A   She ignored her parents' advice.
    B   She chose the subject she was best at in school.
    C   She got better results than she expected.

25 Olivia claims that her success as a business woman is a result of

    A   her university studies.
    B   her natural abilities.
    C   continuous learning through reading.

26 Olivia and her brother sold their soft drinks company because

    A   it was uninteresting.
    B   they were offered jobs overseas.
    C   they wanted to have a long vacation.

27 At the restaurant in Australia, Olivia worked as

    A   a chef.
    B   a waitress.
    C   an assistant manager.

28 What does Olivia say about her working relationship with her brother?

    A   They both work long hours.
    B   She can depend on him.
    C   He never gets upset.

29 According to Olivia, people who own restaurants

    A   have difficulty sleeping.
    B   are stressed by deadlines.
    C   rarely need time on their own.

30 Olivia says that people entering her field of business have to

    A   go through a good recruitment agency.
    B   be interested in all aspects of the food industry.
    C   let others in the business teach them.

You now have 10 minutes to transfer your answers to your Answer Sheet.

SPEAKING   14 minutes

SAMPLE SPEAKING TASKS

PART 1

The interview – about 3 minutes
In this part the interlocutor asks questions to each of the candidates in turn. You
have to give information about yourself and express personal opinions.

PART 2

'Mini presentation' – about 6 minutes
In this part of the test you are asked to give a short talk on a business topic. You
have to choose one of the topics from the three below and then talk for about one
minute. You have one minute to prepare your ideas.

A   WHAT IS IMPORTANT WHEN . . .?

DECIDING WHETHER TO OBTAIN A
FURTHER QUALIFICATION
- TIME COMMITMENT REQUIRED
- CAREER BENEFITS
-

B   WHAT IS IMPORTANT WHEN . . .?

PLACING A NEWSPAPER ADVERTISEMENT

- NEWSPAPER SALES FIGURES
- COST OF ADVERTISING
-

C   WHAT IS IMPORTANT WHEN . . .?
CONSIDERING WHETHER TO INVEST IN
TECHNOLOGY
- BENEFITS TO THE COMPANY
- COSTS INVOLVED
-

PART 3

Discussion – about 5 minutes

In this part of the test you are given a discussion topic. You have 30 seconds to look at the prompt card, an example of which is below, and then about 3 minutes to discuss the topic with your partner. After that the examiner will ask you more questions related to the topic.

For **two** candidates

Work Experience Programme

Your company has decided to offer a 2 week work experience programme for a small group of business students.

You have been asked to help with the preparations for this programme.

Discuss the situation together, and decide:

- what kinds of work experience should be offered to the students
- what information it would be useful to know about the students and how the participants should be selected

---

For **three** candidates

Work Experience Programme

Your company has decided to offer a 2 week work experience programme for a small group of business students.

You have been asked to help with the preparations for this programme.

Discuss the situation together, and decide:

- what kinds of work experience should be offered to the students
- what information it would be useful to know about the students and how the participants should be selected
- what feedback and evaluation should take place after the programme has finished

---

KEY

Test 1   Reading

Part 1

1 D   2 C   3 B   4 D   5 A   6 B
7 A

Part 2

8 D   9 E   10 B   11 A   12 F

Part 3

13 A   14 D   15 C   16 B   17 C
18 B

Part 4

19 A	20 A	21 C	22 D	23 B
24 C	25 B	26 D	27 D	28 B
29 C	30 D	31 C	32 A	33 B

Part 5

34 CORRECT   35 than   36 all
37 give   38 on   39 as   40 qualified
41 CORRECT   42 their   43 be
44 CORRECT   45 for

Test 1   Writing

The following candidate responses were awarded marks in Band 5 (the highest band).

Part 1

To: All staff
From: The Training Manager
Date: 1 March, 2002
Subject: *A Foreign Language Training Course*
I was asked to organise a foreign language training course because of the large export order we received recently. It will start on 15th March. Those who will deal with orders should attend the course.

Part 2

Date: 2 March 2002

Report on Globelink and FTD Shipping Agents

Introduction
The purpose of this report is to present and compare the services of Globelink and FTD as possible new agents for international freight.

Findings
Globelink has 25 years' experience in sea freight worldwide. They offer air freight as well, and we may need that for urgent orders. This company will complete all customs forms and provide all documentations.
    FTD operates mainly in Europe. They offer refrigerated shipping and accept small orders, which would be useful for us. However the charges are a bit higher at FTD than at Globelink.

Conclusions
Choosing Globelink will save us work on customs forms and cost less.

Recommendations
It is recommended that Globelink is chosen due to their international network and documentation service.

Test 1   Listening

Part 1

1 Z/3487/JF
2 pale green
3 BJC 246
4 Special Delivery
5 Marketing
6 International
7 driver / Loboprint driver / company driver
8 night
9 City Council
10 databases
11 graphics
12 Globe Insurance

Part 2

13 F	14 H	15 E	16 C	17 A
18 C	19 B	20 A	21 E	22 H

Part 3

23 B	24 C	25 B	26 B	27 B
28 A	29 C	30 C		

Tapescript

Listening Test One

This is the Business English Certificate, Vantage, Listening Test 1.

Part One. Questions 1 to 12.

You will hear three telephone conversations or messages.

Write one or two words or a number in the numbered spaces on the notes or forms below.

After you have listened once, replay the recording.

Conversation 1.   Questions 1 to 4.

Look at the form below.

You will hear a woman telephoning about some problems with an order.

You have 15 seconds to read through the form.

[pause]

Now listen, and fill in the spaces.

Man: Good afternoon. Stationery Supplies International, Customer Services Department, Michael speaking. How may I help you?

Woman: Oh, hello. My name's Jennifer Gardiner. I'm calling from Fenmore Consultants. It's about the order which we received yesterday.

Man: OK. Please can I have the order number?

Woman: Yes, it's Z/3487/JF. The problem is we've received several incorrect items.

Man: Oh dear, sorry about that. We took on some new staff this week and we've had a few problems. Tell me what's wrong and we'll forward the correct order to you straightaway.

Woman: Good. Well, firstly you sent the wrong size paper. We ordered 100 boxes of A5 paper, not A4. And the envelopes you sent were not the colour we ordered. We wanted pale green, not white.

Man: Right, so that's A5 not A4 paper and pale green envelopes. Anything else?

Woman: Yes. We also ordered 20 printer ink cartridges, that's the TrueJet BJC two four six . . . but you didn't send us any at all.

Man: Oh dear, I'm really sorry. I can only apologise once again and assure you that the correct items will be on their way to you tonight, Special Delivery.

Woman: What shall I do about the things we don't want?

Man: Send them back to us, and we'll refund the full cost.

Woman: Right. Thank you. Goodbye.

Man: Bye bye.

[pause]

Now listen to the recording again.

[pause]

Conversation 2.   Questions 5 to 8.

Look at the note below.

You will hear a man leaving a message on an answering machine.

You have 15 seconds to read through the note.

[pause]

Now listen, and fill in the spaces.

Woman: You have reached the offices of RT Communications. We're sorry there's no one to take your call at the moment. Please leave your message after the tone, stating who the message is for and the date and time of your call. Thank you.

Man: Hi, this is John Castellani from Loboprint. It's Saturday February fourth. This is a message for Joel Frisk, Marketing Department. It's about his visit next week. We've booked him into the International Hotel downtown for four nights – although we checked, and there is still availability for a fifth night if he wants it. Our company driver will meet him at the airport on his arrival. We've arranged for him to give a presentation on RT's digital office system to the Board of Directors on Wednesday morning . . . and then Mr Sachs, the General Manager, has invited him to dinner that evening. Please let us know by midday Monday if you want us to book an extra night at the hotel. We look forward to meeting him. Goodbye!

[pause]

Now listen to the recording again.

[pause]

Conversation 3.   Questions 9 to 12.

Look at the note below.

You will hear a man enquiring about training courses.

You have 15 seconds to read through the note.

[pause]

Now listen, and fill in the spaces.

Woman: Contact Training, how can I help you?

Man: Hello, this is Dave Smith calling from the City Council. I understand you run in-house training courses in word-processing and databases, things like that.

Woman: Yes, are you looking for some training?

Man: Well, yes, we've just taken on some new staff in our department and I'd be interested to know if you have someone who could help them with databases – perhaps a one-week course?

Woman: I'm sure we can.

Man: Good. In addition to that – if it's possible – we have some other staff who need some individual training, but that would be in graphics.

Woman: Oh yes, we do graphics courses. Did someone recommend us to you?

Man: Yes, a friend of mine at Globe Insurance . . .

Woman: Oh yes, we put on a course for them a few months ago.

Man: They were very impressed . . .

Woman: Good! Well, I'll just take a few details

[pause]

Now listen to the recording again.

[pause]

That is the end of Part One. You now have 20 seconds to check your answers.

[pause]

Part Two. Questions 13–22.

Section 1. Questions 13–17.

You will hear five short recordings.

For each recording, decide what the speaker's job is.

Write one letter (A–H) next to the number of the recording.

Do not use any letter more than once.

After you have listened once, replay each recording.

You have 15 seconds to read the list A–H.

[pause]

Now listen, and decide what each speaker's job is.

[pause]

Thirteen

Man: We've been working on this new circuit for a long time and we're sure that it's ready for production now. As you know, it took a while to find a solution to the problems we had with the old circuit. The diagrams on the second page'll give you a rough idea of how it works and what's different about it. I'll explain the ideas behind it in a minute, and then I'll hand over to Mark for any questions about manufacturing costs, and then maybe we can agree on a start date for production.

[pause]

Fourteen

Man: Hello, it's Paul Fields, here. We spoke yesterday. I'm calling about the forms you filled in for the loan. They arrived this morning but there are some more figures that I'll need before we can do anything. Your company's projected figures only cover next year, but we'll need them for three years. The rest is fine . . . so if you could get those to me in the next week, then once our legal people have checked everything out, I'll be able to authorise the loan.

[pause]

Fifteen

Woman: Hello, it's Sheila Griffiths here from The Haverbridge. I'm ringing to check the dates that you booked for the Advertiser's Convention. The problem is that we seem to have two different dates; the publicity materials that you sent have the 14th down as the starting date, yet in your original letter to us, you booked the 15th to the 18th. Those dates are fixed now and I'm afraid it's not possible to change them.

[pause]

Sixteen

Man: There can be a problem when the packaging on a retailer's own brand is similar to other leading brands. There's a court case I'm preparing at the moment which is about just this problem. Until it's finished, I think the marketing department should be very careful in this area, and stick to completely new designs for our own brand packaging. That way we can avoid the risk of damages.

[pause]

Seventeen

Woman: Hello, it's Rachel Lister here from Cross & Taylor. I got your letter accepting the post this morning. I'm just ringing to arrange a time for us to meet and sign your contract. Your departmental manager has asked me to go through it with you – and to answer any questions you have about holidays and the pension scheme and so on. I should be able to take you over to the sales department afterwards, so you can meet some of your future colleagues.

[pause]

Section 2. Questions 18–22.

You will hear another five recordings. Each speaker is leaving a message on an answering machine.

For each recording, decide what the main reason is for the phone call.

Write one letter (A–H) next to the number of the recording.

Do not use any letter more than once.

After you have listened once, replay each recording.

You have 15 seconds to read the list A–H.

[pause]

Now listen, and decide what the main reason is for each phone call.

[pause]

Eighteen

Woman: Tom it's Paula. Just checking you haven't forgotten the presentation we agreed to do. Do you realise it's only ten days away? To be honest, I'm beginning to regret offering to do it. Expect you are too . . . Anyway I'll be in touch early next week, so we can start preparing properly.

[pause]

Nineteen

Woman: It's Elena . . . Sorry to bother you on your first day off but I'm trying to order that software you were talking about yesterday – you know, for processing customer complaints? The suppliers need to know the exact name of the package and the company that produces it – it seems there's more than one on the market. Can you help? Give me a ring at the office before 4 o'clock if you can. Otherwise, have a good break.

[pause]

Twenty

Man: Mike this is Bob Richards from Birmingham Traders here. Look, today's delivery is not much better than last week's . . . it looks like your process needs looking at again. Basically, you're not getting the printing areas of the 2 colours right – there's this strange optical effect instead of a clear diagram in 2 colours. Could you give me a ring when you get in?

[pause]

Twenty-one

Woman: Hi, it's Margaret – just a quick word to say I thought the presentation was great – you deserve a bonus, in my opinion. I mean, answering those difficult questions on accounting procedures when it's not really your field at all . . . Well, I know I couldn't have done it! My one complaint is that the coffee-break was so short! Bye!

[pause]

Twenty-two

Nick: Mark, just a quick message – I'm on the way to the station. I've thought about our discussion at this afternoon's meeting and I think the research people do need to be involved, and right now. So can you set up a meeting with them for when I get back, say Thursday or Friday? Can you also send them an agenda based on what we discussed today? Thanks.

[pause]

Now listen to the recording again.

That is the end of Part Two.

[pause]

Part Three. Questions 23–30.

You will hear an interview on local radio with Dr Tim Carter, the author of a book on how to give effective business presentations.

For each question 23–30, mark one letter (A, B or C) for the correct answer.

After you have listened once, replay the recording.

You have 45 seconds to read through the questions.

[pause]

Now listen, and mark A, B or C.

[pause]

Woman: Welcome to 'Mid Afternoon,' Dr Carter. Now, I imagine you're here in Birmingham to promote your recently published book 'The Art of Giving Presentations'. Is that right?

Man: Well, not really, no! In fact the book isn't really recent at all – it came out at the beginning of last year. I'm actually here this week to give a series of talks outlining some ideas I've had since then.

Woman: So are these ideas the basis for your next book?

Man: Well, it's really too early to talk about that!

Woman: I see. Now tell me, how did you become involved in this particular area of communication skills?

Man: Well, many years ago, as a young sales executive, I had to give presentations, but I felt I wasn't doing them very well. My boss never actually criticised me, and my colleagues weren't doing any better than me, but the point was that *I* didn't feel satisfied with my performance. You see, if I'm doing something, I have to do it well.

Woman: So you decided to do something about improving your performance.

Man: That's right. I tried to find some books to help me but there weren't really any available in those days . . . so I eventually decided on a totally practical approach: I tried to find out what my problem was by studying the way the best speakers gave presentations, by talking to them, even watching them prepare. Then I compared their performance with mine.

Woman: And what was your main problem? Nervousness? I know that's mine.

Man: Well I had always *thought* it was nervousness, and it's true that at the time I had no techniques for dealing with that. But I think audiences accept the fact that speakers get nervous, and it really doesn't matter. No, I discovered that my No. 1 problem was *preparation*. Nobody had ever told me anything

about how to prepare, and I didn't really know how to do it properly.

Woman: And when you realised that, what did you change?

Man: Well, before, I used to go through the whole presentation in an empty room on my own. The first change in my approach came when I realised it's much more realistic and much more useful to do it in front of two or three colleagues. That way you get some feedback. Otherwise you have no idea whether or not your presentation is effective, or which parts might need further attention.

Woman: Is that the method you recommend now?

Man: Well, not quite. What I would advise is to make a video of your practice presentation . . .

Woman: Instead of using colleagues?

Man: No, a recording of your presentation to them. Then it's easier for all of you to go back and see what's wrong and how it can be improved. It's actually much better than recording other people doing real presentations, however good they are.

Woman: So that's the preparation, but are there any factors which make the presentation itself difficult, even if you are prepared?

Man: Well obviously, yes. Some speakers *imagine*, quite wrongly, that every audience is unfriendly, at least at the beginning. And this affects their performance. And then there may be a few people who worry about their lack of experience of public speaking. But really what bothers most speakers is things like the OHP and the microphone – are they going to work, and so on.

Woman: Are there any techniques that are effective for overcoming feelings of anxiety?

Man: Well, first I have to say that some people never manage to reduce their anxiety levels. What they *can* do is learn to relax their face muscles while they speak, so that they look relaxed, even though they feel just as anxious as before. In order to really reduce anxiety, some experts recommend concentrating on something that you enjoyed recently – but I find this is hopeless . . . I just forget what I was about to say! For me though, what has worked is some simple breathing exercises, breathing in deeply and slowly while making a pause. This definitely slows down the heart rate. That's what I would try first of all.

Woman: Something we can all try – Dr Carter, thank you very much indeed.

[pause]

Now listen to the recording again.

[pause]

That is the end of Part Three. You now have ten minutes to transfer your answers to your Answer Sheet. Stop here and time ten minutes.

Test 2   Reading

Part 1

1 D   2 C   3 A   4 B   5 C   6 D
7 B

Part 2

8 F   9 E   10 C   11 A   12 D

Part 3

13 D   14 A   15 B   16 D   17 B
18 A

Part 4

19 B	20 D	21 A	22 B	23 C
24 D	25 B	26 A	27 B	28 C
29 D	30 B	31 D	32 A	33 C

Part 5

34 is   35 with   36 CORRECT
37 CORRECT   38 between   39 from
40 CORRECT   41 what   42 CORRECT
43 the   44 of   45 if

Test 2   Writing

The following candidate responses were awarded marks in band 5 (the highest band).

Part 1

To: Nick Johnson

Subject: Presentation Skills Seminar

I would like to attend a seminar on 3rd April.
It is about presentation skills. Since I have to make many presentations to customers, this seminar will be very useful.
Could you tell me if it's possible to take time off work to attend the seminar?

Thanks

Angela

Part 2

Report on recent developments in the market of sports goods

INTRODUCTION
This report aims to assess current and future situation in sports goods market.

FINDINGS
At present, our greatest market is North America, where we sell about 44% of our goods. It is followed by Europe (26%), South America (19%) and Asia/Pacific (11%).
If we compare our results with competitors, we can see that in year 2002 we have become the second largest retailer with a turnover of $60 million, whereas in year 2001 we were in third place with $40 million. We are the only company which succeded in increasing its turnover in year 2002.

CONCLUSION
In order to continue this positive development we have decided to change our present sales distribution in the year 2003. We intend to increase our turnover in Europe by 4% with 6 new stores, in Asia/Pacific by 3% with 4 new stores and in South America by 4% with 3 new stores.
Therefore we will decrease our sales in North America, where the market is already saturated. All these changes should boost our turnover by 15% in year 2003 and thus we might become the greatest retailer in the market.

Test 2   Listening

Part 1

1 advertising campaign
2 (Thursday) 2(nd) May
3 Boardroom
4 30
5 Black
6 (the) builder
7 Friday
8 (the/your/his) plans
9 Personnel
10 programming/programing
11 application form
12 2 hours

Part 2

13 G	14 B	15 H	16 A	17 C
18 D	19 F	20 A	21 B	22 E

Part 3

23 C	24 B	25 A	26 C	27 C
28 A	29 A	30 B		

Tapescript

Listening Test Two

This is the Business English Certificate, Vantage Listening Test 2.

Part One. Questions 1 to 12.

You will hear three telephone conversations.

Write one or two words or a number in the numbered spaces on the notes or forms below.

After you have listened once, replay the recording.

Conversation 1. Questions 1 to 4.

Look at the form below.

You will hear a man making a request for catering.

You have 15 seconds to read through the form.

[pause]

Now listen, and fill in the spaces.

Woman: Hello, Executive Catering Services, Anna speaking. How can I help you?

Man: Hello Anna, this is Julian Russell from Family Holidays. I wondered if you could do some catering for us next week. We're having a small reception – it's to launch a new advertising campaign. Would you be free?

Woman: When exactly is it, Mr Russell?

Man: Next Thursday – that's May the second.

Woman: Oh yes, I can do that. Where will you be holding it?

Man: We thought we'd have it at Head Office and use the Boardroom because there's enough room for everyone there.

Woman: OK. What sort of things would you like?

Man: Just a light lunch, I think, so that people can eat while they move around and talk to each other. You did something similar for us last year – we'd be happy to have the same menu again.

Woman: Right, I'll look in my diary and see what you had. Oh, I nearly forgot to ask you, how many should I cater for?

Man: Well, I think most people will be able to come. Perhaps around 25. No, let's say 30 to be sure.

Woman: Right. Thank you for getting in touch, Mr Russell, I'll send you confirmation of the arrangements by the end of the week and then I'll . . .

[pause]

Now listen to the recording again.

[pause]

Conversation 2. Questions 5–8.

Look at the notes below.

You will hear a man calling to change an arrangement.

You have 15 seconds to read through the notes.

[pause]

Now listen, and fill in the spaces.

Woman: Hello, Production department, can I help you?

Man: This is Bob Black from Planning. Is Sam Wong there?

Woman: I'm afraid he's out all day on a visit. Can I take a message?

Man: Yes, please, if you would. It's about the meeting we scheduled for Wednesday.

Woman: Oh yes, about the new factory site . . .

Man: That's right. I've just heard from the builder that he can't come on Wednesday. I wonder if we can change the date.

Woman: That shouldn't be a problem. I'll just look in Mr Wong's diary. Right, I've cancelled Wednesday's meeting.

Man: OK, now how's he fixed on Friday . . .?

Woman: He's got a meeting at nine-thirty but that should be finished by ten-fifteen. What time did you have in mind?

Man: Well, the two of us can come any time that morning, so could we make it 11 o'clock?

Woman: That sounds fine.

Man: We want to discuss the new production units, so could you ask Sam to bring his plans with him.

Woman: Yes, certainly.

Man: Thanks a lot, bye.

[pause]

Now listen to the recording again.

[pause]

Conversation 3. Questions 9–12.

Look at the note below.

You will hear two colleagues talking on the phone.

You have 15 seconds to read through the note.

[pause]

Now listen, and fill in the spaces.

Woman: Good morning – IT here.
Man: Hi, Joanne, it's Dave Proctor here from Personnel.
Woman: Hello Dave.
Man: Joanne, I've got someone here with me who's just had an interview with us. We're pretty impressed with him and I think he might be the sort of person you're looking for for the programming post.
Woman: OK. There's nobody around to talk to him at the moment. I'll leave a message for Tom, asking him to come over and see you as soon as he gets back.
Man: Sure. Could you ask him to bring an application form for your department when he comes? This candidate hasn't applied directly to you and I think perhaps he should. You'd get a lot more information on his relevant experience.
Woman: OK. Is he employed at the moment . . . I mean does he need to get away now or can he wait? It might be half an hour or so . . .
Man: Well, he says he can stay for another two hours so there's plenty of time. But he can't wait any longer, as he's got a train to catch.
Woman: I understand. We won't keep him waiting that long. Now, if you could just give me his name . . .

[pause]

Now listen to the recording again.

[pause]

That is the end of Part One. You now have 20 seconds to check your answers.

[pause]

Part Two. Questions 13–22.

Section 1. Questions 13–17.

You will hear five people talking about giving presentations.

For each recording, decide what advice the speaker is giving.

Write one letter (A–H) next to the number of the recording.

Do not use any letter more than once.

After you have listened once, replay each recording.

You have 15 seconds to read the list A–H.

[pause]

Now listen, and decide what advice each speaker is giving.

[pause]

Thirteen

Man: Obviously you can't force people to be interested, but they can go away saying 'That was a really good presentation' and how do you do that? Well, for me, the golden rule is, don't run over time. Whatever it is you want to say and however much time you have to say it in, as soon as your time is up, stop. You only lose them after that!

[pause]

Fourteen

Woman: I'd advise making a clear outline of what you want to say beforehand on paper . . . to make sure you don't forget anything. Then categorise the points and come up with words – like a code – that'll remind you about what you want to say. Then practise it as much as you can, so that in the end you hardly have to look down and the audience can see your face.

[pause]

Fifteen

Man: I've been in this business for years and I think I can safely say I'm good at it. Not because I've got fancy visual aids, not because I've got a wardrobe full of designer suits – not me! – and certainly not because I have stacks of little note cards. People love my talks and you know why – they do the talking! That's the key.

[pause]

Sixteen

Woman: You know that some people will be there because they want to be and some will be there because they have to be. So it helps if you start with a joke or something that captures their attention, and if you stop on a high note as well, you'll find most people go away feeling good. If you find you've got time left, you can use that for questions from the audience.

[pause]

Seventeen

Man: I always end up saying too much, but I think you only get one chance to say it sometimes, so better too much than too little. What helps enormously is to be clever about how you use the OHP. Anything I put on the OHP has got to be simple and easy to read, so that it helps the listeners. Diagrams, especially, have to be large enough for the audience to see.

[pause]

Section 2. Questions 18–22.

You will hear another five short recordings. Each speaker is talking on the phone.

For each recording, decide the main reason for the call.

Write one letter (A–H) next to the number of the recording.

Do not use any letter more than once.

After you have listened once, replay each recording.

You have 15 seconds to read the list of reasons A–H.

[pause]

Now listen, and decide the reason for each speaker's call.

[pause]

Eighteen

Woman: Good morning. I'm calling about your advertisement in Stationery News looking for overseas distributors. Could you send me some more details about this, as I'm very interested in this opportunity. My name is Sally Brown, and the address is . . .

[pause]

Nineteen

Man: Hello. We bought a photocopying machine from you last week, but we're having a few problems with it. I don't think we've worked

out how to use it properly yet. Do you think you could send someone round to show us how it works, please?

[pause]

Twenty

Woman: Hello. I'm thinking about placing an advertisement in your Classified Section, but I've got a question. What I'd like to know is whether you think an advertisement in bold would be more effective. I know they're more expensive, but in your experience, is it worth the extra money?

[pause]

Twenty-one

Woman: Hello, Mandy. You know that report we were talking about yesterday? Well, I faxed you a copy of it in the afternoon but I'm afraid some of the pages were wrong. I was working on another report at the same time and, somehow, some of the pages got mixed up. I'm not sure how it happened, but what I'll do is, I'll fax you a new copy now. I hope this hasn't caused any problems.

[pause]

Twenty-two

Man: Good morning. I ordered some paper from you a week ago and you promised to send it to me immediately. It should have been here by now, but I haven't received it. This is really unacceptable. I shall have to find another supplier if you can't deliver on time.

[pause]

That is the end of Part Two.

[pause]

Part Three. Questions 23–30.

You will hear an interview with Susan Gates, Director of Human Resources policy at Robertson's, a national chain of supermarkets. She recently sat on a government committee that looked into the funding of higher education.

For each question 23–30, mark one letter (A, B or C) for the correct answer.

After you have listened once, replay the recording.

You have 45 seconds to read through the questions.

[pause]

Now listen, and mark A, B or C.

[pause]

Man: Perhaps I can begin by asking you why you think it's important for business leaders to be involved in higher education?

Woman: Well, although most graduates still enter the teaching profession, an increasing number are employed by the business community – this is a major destination for new graduates. So it's only natural that we should want to have a say in higher education, the courses that are being offered, and so on.

Man: And why do you think the supermarket chain, Robertson's, needed to be represented on the government committee?

Woman: Well, about 50% of jobs that come onto the market don't require a specific degree, so they're known as non-specialist. This area's made up mostly of the service and retail sectors, with the retail sector alone accounting for 11% of graduate jobs. The high-tech industries, for example, IT and manufacturing, were already represented on the committee, and we thought that the opinions of the non-specialist employer, like Robertson's, should also be taken into account.

Man: What about the findings of the committee? What was important to you there?

Woman: Well, firstly, that employers are looking for more than a body of knowledge. In today's world, the knowledge that a student gains has a short life span – it won't necessarily be relevant in 20 years' time. The committee recognised that higher education needs to take on board the fact that employers are looking for important, universal skills – in particular, those of communication, numeracy and IT.

Man: So what role do these skills have?

Woman: Well, take numeracy. The sort of people who reach the upper levels of organisations are all highly numerate. They have the ability to work with numbers at a very sophisticated level. So it's important that people can understand numbers and spot a mistake very, very quickly – even if there are a lot of noughts at the end.

Man: What other findings of the committee were important to you?

Woman: Another finding was recognising the importance of work experience. I think it's true to say that graduates with work experience are much more likely to get a job than those without. At Robertson's we employ 25,000 students throughout the country and we're looking to increase that. We need people with experience of working with others – this makes a big difference. Oh, and the third important finding was recognising the importance of applied research. One problem is the gap between the discovery of certain innovations and actually putting them into practice. That's where, as a country, we don't do as well as some of our competitors. We've got a wonderful record for pure research but it isn't translated into economic growth. That's where we need to build better links between business and industry, and higher education.

Man: And do you think these findings are equally important for small businesses?

Woman: Yes, even more so. Small businesses jdon't have time to train people to the extent that large organisations do. It's particularly important to them that graduates have the skills to go into the workplace and make a contribution right from the start. I think the key skills that we've already talked about, together with work experience, are very helpful in that situation.

Man: And finally, what should the business community and the world of higher education be aiming for in the future?

Woman: We need to work more in partnership and that requires effort, I think, on both sides. Business leaders could invest more time in higher education, for example sitting on higher education councils, collaborating on research. Some of this goes on already, but more links are needed. And while business solutions don't apply exactly to higher education, we still have a lot to offer in terms of the management of change.

Man: Susan Gates – thank you for coming to the studio to talk to us.

[pause]

Now listen to the recording again.

[pause]

That is the end of Part Three. You now have ten minutes to transfer your answers to your Answer Sheet. Stop here and time ten minutes.

Test 3   Reading

Part 1

1 C   2 A   3 D   4 B   5 B   6 C
7 A

Part 2

8 C   9 F   10 A   11 E   12 B

Part 3

13 A   14 C   15 A   16 B   17 B
18 D

Part 4

19 C	20 B	21 C	22 D	23 A
24 B	25 D	26 A	27 B	28 C
29 D	30 B	31 D	32 A	33 C

Part 5

34 without   35 us   36 CORRECT
37 CORRECT   38 to   39 that
40 against   41 CORRECT   42 since
43 this   44 CORRECT   45 lot

Test 3   Writing

The following candidate responses were awarded
marks in band 5 (the highest band).

Part 1

Fri 7th of October

Dave

A quick note to let you know that I'm going to
London next month. Could you please book a
flight to London 12/11 and the return 15/11?
Please make a reservation at the Stage Hotel for
me.

Maria

Part 2

Dear Mrs Geddings

I write regarding a training course on health and
safety which I attended 27 November.
When I booked this course, I chose your company
as it came highly recommended and the courses
seemed to be of a high standard. I was promised
an experienced trainer but unfortunately he was
sick and the replacement was not as good as

expected. Regarding the information packs these
were only a pile of loose photocopies, which was
not promised. The class was supposed to be
about 8 people but in mine there were about 15.
Finally, I should make it clear that the class started
1 hour late, and the lunch that was served, was
cold.
I am sure you can understand my disappointment.
I would therefore be glad if you could investigate
this matter.
I look forward to hearing from you.

Yours sincerely

Lisa Kostevska
Cabin Attendent

Test 3   Listening

Part 1

1 computers
2 technician
3 install
4 553106
5 Accounts
6 job offer
7 (his) pension
8 Friday (morning)
9 clothing range
10 payment terms
11 20,000
12 January 30th / 30(th) January

Part 2

| 13 E | 14 C | 15 H | 16 A | 17 G |
| 18 E | 19 D | 20 H | 21 F | 22 A |

Part 3

| 23 C | 24 B | 25 C | 26 A | 27 B |
| 28 A | 29 B | 30 C | | |

Tapescript

Listening Test Three

*This is the Business English Certificate, Vantage
Listening Test 3.*

Part One. Questions 1 to 12.

*You will hear three telephone conversations or
messages.*

*Write one or two words or a number in the
numbered spaces on the notes or forms below.*

After you have listened once, replay the recording.

Conversation 1.   Questions 1 to 4.

Look at the note below.

You will hear a man making a call about a delivery.

You have 15 seconds to read through the note.

[pause]

Now listen, and fill in the spaces.

Woman: Good morning. Sales Department.

Man: Hello. Could I speak to John White?

Woman: He's not in the office today, I'm afraid. He's in London for a conference. Would you like to leave a message for him?

Man: Yes, I think I'd better. This is Patrick Fisher from A & L Systems. I wanted to tell John that the computers he ordered will be arriving tomorrow.

Woman: Oh, yes. He's been expecting them to arrive this week.

Man: Will he be in the office tomorrow?

Woman: Yes, he should be back. It's only a one-day conference.

Man: It's just that he'll have to speak to the technician who'll be coming out to see you. Her name is Sarah Robbins, she'll be arriving about 10 o'clock and she'll need to be told where to install the computers. I haven't been given any instructions, and anyway, it's much easier to sort that out on the day.

Woman: OK, I'll leave the message on his desk so that he gets it first thing tomorrow morning.

Man: If there are any problems, I'll be in the office tomorrow and he can ring me. The number's 55 31 06.

Woman: OK. Thanks for ringing. Goodbye.

Man: Goodbye.

[pause]

Now listen to the recording again.

[pause]

Conversation 2.   Questions 5–8.

Look at the note below.

You will hear a man telephoning his personnel officer.

You have 15 seconds to read through the note.

[pause]

Now listen, and fill in the spaces.

Woman: Human Resources, Mary speaking. Can I help you?

Man: Oh good morning. I'd like to speak to Peter Robinson, please.

Woman: I'm afraid Mr Robinson's out of the office at the moment.

Man: I see. It's Roshan Singh here, from Accounts. I really need to speak to him fairly urgently.

Woman: He's not going to be back until Thursday. I'm his Personal Assistant, maybe I can help you.

Man: OK. The thing is I've had a very attractive job offer.

Woman: Oh, congratulations. Where is it?

Man: Well, I don't want to say too much about it right now, but it would be a promotion and the pay and conditions are very good. The trouble is I need to speak to Mr Robinson about my pension before I make a final decision.

Woman: I tell you what I'll do. I'll give him a message as soon as he gets in on Thursday morning.

Man: If you could, I'd be grateful, because I've got to give them an answer by Friday morning.

Woman: All right. I've made a note of that. I'll contact you as soon as I've spoken to him on Thursday.

Man: Thanks a lot.

[pause]

Now listen to the recording again.

[pause]

Conversation 3.   Questions 9–12.

Look at the notes below.

You will hear a woman calling a company about a possible order.

You have 15 seconds to read through the notes.

[pause]

Now listen, and fill in the spaces.

Man: Good morning. Adventure Holidays Equipment Ltd. Philip Sykes speaking.

Woman: Good morning, Mr Sykes, it's Julie Ventnor from Polareach Ltd. I spoke to you briefly last week and you sent us your brochure.

Man: That's right. Was it useful?

Woman: Well, we're not really interested in the tents and other equipment, but we may want to order from your clothing range.

Man: Oh right. Have you got one of our order forms?

Woman: Yes, but first I need some information on the payment terms. These are quite important because, as I think I said last time, we're interested in purchasing quite large quantities.

Man: Right. What sort of quantities are you thinking of?

Woman: We'll want about two thousand pounds worth of goods for each of our ten stores, so we'll probably be giving you orders of around twenty thousand pounds a month.

Man: I'm very pleased to hear that. Can I send the information to you later today?

Woman: That'll be fine. Thanks.

Man: If the terms are acceptable, may I suggest a meeting towards the end of January?

Woman: Yes, that would be good. Let me see. I can do the 23^(rd) or the 30^(th).

Man: The 23^(rd)'s no good for me, I'm afraid.

Woman: Let's say January the 30^(th) then. I'll be in touch at a later date to confirm the time.

Man: OK, that's fine. Bye.

Woman: Bye.

[pause]

Now listen to the recording again.

[pause]

That is the end of Part One. You now have 20 seconds to check your answers.

[pause]

Part Two. Questions 13–22.

Section 1. Questions 13–17.

You will hear five short recordings. Each speaker is saying what a manager must do to achieve success.

For each recording, decide which is the most important action for that speaker.

Write one letter (A–H) next to the number of the recording.

Do not use any letter more than once.

After you have listened once, replay each recording.

You have 15 seconds to read the list A–H.

[pause]

Now listen, and decide which is the most important action for each speaker.

[pause]

Thirteen

Woman: Well, if you don't know what your aims are, how can you achieve anything? The secret is to decide what your priorities are first. Of course, it's essential that everyone in your team knows what you're aiming for. Then you can work out a plan of action to reach these aims.

[pause]

Fourteen

Man: We all know how plans can fail to fit reality within weeks. The only way to overcome problems is to make sure you've got all the necessary information about the particular situation. Once you have a good understanding of all aspects of the problem, then it becomes clearer what needs to be done next.

[pause]

Fifteen

Man: I don't believe in spending too much time finding and analysing every possible solution to a problem. Success depends on one thing and one thing alone: getting things done as soon as possible. Once you've decided what to do, take immediate action and work out the details later – that's my rule. If I waited until I had all the information available, I wouldn't get anywhere.

[pause]

Sixteen

Woman: Don't forget that organisations are made up of individuals with their own interests. And they often use information and plans to further their own aims. Politics and differences in opinion are common in large firms. So as I see it, a manager's main role is to solve problems and differences between team members in a way that everyone can accept.

[pause]

Seventeen

Woman: Achieving success is simpler than we all think. Above all, a manager needs to make sure that everyone is clear about what it is that their post involves. Every employee needs to know exactly what their functions and their responsibilities are. Then that's one less thing to worry about, and they can get on with their work.

[pause]

Section 2. Questions 18–22.

You will hear another five recordings. Each speaker is talking about a visitor to the office.

For each recording, decide which visitor the speaker is talking about. Write one letter (A–H) next to the number of the recording.

Do not use any letter more than once.

After you have listened once, replay each recording.

You have 15 seconds to read the list A–H.

[pause]

Now listen, and decide which visitor each speaker is talking about.

[pause]

Eighteen

Man: The thing is, he was a very good customer of ours until about five years ago, when we had that safety problem with the R21. He didn't reply to our literature or anything for all that time, and then suddenly there's this phonecall: 'I'll be in England next week. Could I arrange to come and see you sometime?' I think he'll like the present range, so let's hope we can get back to normal business relations . . .

[pause]

Nineteen

Woman: What he wants to interview us about is our new annual travel insurance packages. As you know, they're selling pretty well at the moment . . . so the competition is getting worried. Anyway, after interviewing me, he's going to talk to the MD and then he wants a photograph. The article's coming out in next month's issue.

[pause]

Twenty

Man: Apparently, the company she represents is part of a big American chain and they can offer some better deals on the kind of foreign trip we have to go on, especially on hotels. The fact is, I don't think our usual people have been doing a particularly good job, so this will be some healthy competition. Anyway, she's coming here at 4.

[pause]

Twenty-one

Man: As far as I can understand, she's come across some problems with the ownership of the land. The owners of part of the site can't find the relevant papers. She wants to check our insurance policies, too – you see, we may be able to claim if we have to postpone the move for legal reasons . . . Oh, and there are some documents we've got to sign for her . . . so we may need you as a witness.

[pause]

Twenty-two

Woman: I quite liked him, actually. He didn't ask as many questions as the one who came last time, but he was thorough. There were a few problems with the latest legal requirements regarding electrical equipment – leaving cables lying around with the plug in the socket, that sort of thing . . . but nothing too serious . . . There's no reason why we shouldn't get a reasonable report again.

[pause]

That is the end of Part Two.

[pause]

Part Three. Questions 23–30.

You will hear a radio interview with Richard Wood, the founder of Bookstore, a company that sells books on the internet.

For each question 23–30, mark one letter (A, B or C) for the correct answer.

After you have listened once, replay the recording.

You have 45 seconds to read through the questions.

[pause]

Now listen, and mark A, B or C.

[pause]

Woman: Good morning, Richard. Now, in 1994 you were a computer science graduate with a good job working for an investment company . . . and then you started Bookstore. Why?

Man: Well, I was thirty and settled at work, but then I came across a report predicting annual internet growth at 2,300%. The figure was like an alarm clock ringing in my head. I started to think about the regrets I might have at eighty. I realised I probably wouldn't even remember the things that seemed important in my thirties (like getting my end-of-year pay bonus. But I'd definitely tell myself I'd been a fool to ignore the internet.

Woman: How did you go about choosing a product?

Man: Well, I drew up a list of twenty products, from clothes to gardening tools, and from that I got a shortlist of five, and then I assessed them. I thought about market growth in different countries and I also did some research into suppliers. But there were other important factors as well. I wanted a product that didn't retail for too high a figure. I thought that since many people would be buying from the internet for the first time, they might be afraid to take a risk with large amounts of money.

Woman: And what made you decide on books?

Man: Well, basically, I found out that books had an eighty-two billion dollar market world-wide. There's also a high demand for CDs – a product I nearly went for – but with books there's a much wider choice. There're 3 million items in the book category, but only 300,000 in CDs. This choice meant the capabilities of the computer – in organisation and selection – could be put to good use.

Woman: Bookstore has certainly been very successful. Why do you think that is?

Man: Well, it's not been easy. For the first five years, it was a struggle raising funds and developing the right software. The ideas weren't the difficult bit. If you and I sat down here for an hour, we'd come up with a hundred good ideas. The hard bit is making those ideas work. There are several key elements, which for me were research, recruiting the right staff, and prioritising.

Woman: And you're satisfied with your customer growth?

Man: Well, it was a bit slow at first but then it picked up and from May '97 we started to see our greatest growth. We went from a hundred and twenty million dollars annual sales revenue to two hundred and thirty million dollars by the end of that year, and from 340,000 customers to 15 million. 58% of them were repeat customers. By '98, sales had reached almost three hundred and ten million dollars.

Woman: And is Bookstore's success reflected in its profits?

Man: Well, at the moment we're focusing on introducing ourselves to customers and we spend a lot on advertising. Anything else would be a poor management decision. But, of course, it's reflected in our final figures. It's not unusual for a four-year-old company like ours to be in an investment cycle. What is more unusual is for a young company like Bookstore to be sold on the stock market, which happened in July '97.

Woman: Bookstore is well-known for its high-quality customer service. What is the secret of your success in this area?

Man: Well, firstly our books are delivered fast and any complaints are dealt with by email and what's important is that the email is always answered in a friendly way, with the emphasis on 'the customer is always right'. In fact, customers sometimes feel guilty about complaining because Bookstore staff are so helpful! Regular customers are recognised when they go to our website, and we suggest titles to them, based on their previous purchases.

Woman: Do you think Bookstore offers a better service than its competitors?

Man: Well, yes. We'd been in the market for about two years before most of our competitors started so we had a head start and although some have caught up now, we're still cheaper. Our book price includes tax and delivery. Most of our competitors' prices don't. But what's more important is that Bookstore has a talented, hard-working staff. As an incentive, everyone's offered shares in the company and this helps to create a sense of ownership. We provide a better service because of that.

Woman: Thank you, Richard. It was very interesting to talk to you . . .

[pause]

Now listen to the recording again.

[pause]

That is the end of Part Three. You now have ten minutes to transfer your answers to your Answer Sheet. Stop here and time ten minutes.

Test 4　Reading

Part 1

1 B	2 C	3 D	4 A	5 C	6 B
7 D					

Part 2

8 C   9 A   10 F   11 D   12 E

Part 3

13 A   14 B   15 C   16 C   17 D
18 D

Part 4

19 C   20 A   21 D   22 A   23 D
24 C   25 B   26 A   27 D   28 D
29 A   30 A   31 B   32 C   33 C

Part 5

34 such   35 CORRECT   36 by
37 the   38 to   39 CORRECT
40 those   41 it   42 that
43 CORRECT   44 in   45 all

Test 4   Writing

The following candidates responses were awarded marks in Band 5 (the highest band).

Part 1

To: Anna Jay

Subject: Talk Next Friday

I would like to give the talk suggested by you and I think 9.30 am, after the break, would be the perfect time.
Required equipment: - Overhead Projector
                    - Flipchart with Pens

Please give me some information about the people participating.

Renate

Part 2

22 July

Dear Ms Brown

Subject: New premises

With reference to your advertisement in the Local newspaper, we would like to have more information about the above.
Could you tell us which other firms are in the area, and what are the sizes of the units available for rental.
Regarding the financial help mentioned, could you

inform us who would qualify for it and how to apply.
Another point to clarify is the skilled labour costs compared with other areas.
Finally, we would be grateful if you could send us the information pack to our address.
We look forward to hearing from you soon.

Yours sincerely

Alya Maideen

Test 4   Listening

Part 1

1 Regional Organiser/Organizer
2 J1856R
3 (the) staff newsletter
4 Sales (Department/Dept)
5 (the) Financial Director
6 45630421
7 debit
8 cheques/checks
9 (the) Management
10 Tower
11 buffet (lunch)
12 equipment

Part 2

13 H   14 F   15 A   16 G   17 E
18 E   19 H   20 D   21 B   22 C

Part 3

23 B   24 A   25 B   26 A   27 C
28 B   29 C   30 C

Tapescript

Listening Test Four

This is the Business English Certificate, Vantage Listening Test 4.

Part One. Questions 1 to 12.

You will hear three telephone conversations or messages.

Write one or two words or a number in the numbered spaces on the notes or forms below.

After you have listened once, replay the recording.

Conversation 1.   Questions 1 to 4.

Look at the notes below.

You will hear a man phoning for a job application form.

You have 15 seconds to read through the form.

[pause]

Now listen, and fill in the spaces.

Woman: This is the Personnel Department of CJ Productions. Please state the title and reference number of the job you're phoning about and state where you saw the advert. Please give your name and address clearly.

Man: Hello. I'm phoning about one of the jobs going in the Marketing Department. It's the Regional Organiser's job in that department which I'm interested in. The reference number quoted in the ad is J-1-8-5-6-R. This is an internal request – I saw the advertisement you put in the staff newsletter. Please send the application form and information pack to me, Daniel Johnson – in the Sales Department. Thank you.

[pause]

Now listen to the recording again.

[pause]

Conversation 2. Questions 5–8.

Look at the notes below.

You will hear a man telephoning a bank about a problem with an account.

You have 15 seconds to read through the notes.

[pause]

Now listen, and fill in the spaces.

Woman: Good morning – HPR Bank. Customer Services Division. How may I help you?

Man: Good morning. My name's George Bliss. I'm the Financial Director of Arundel Holdings. I've got a query on our business account.

Woman: Just a moment. I'll get it up on screen. Can you give me the account number?

Man: Certainly. It's 456 – 30 – 421.

Woman: And your identification code?

Man: Hamlet.

Woman: Right, Mr Bliss. What's the problem?

Man: Well, I received a statement from you this morning and there's a difference between that and our records. The statement shows a debit of £15,000 on June 10th, but no one here signed

anything for that amount, so I'd like to know what's going on.

Woman: Yes, mmm, here it is – £15,000. That's odd. It says cheque number 3-0-6-9-8-4.

Man: Yes, I can see that on the statement, but that can't be right. All our cheques begin with 5-0. It's not one of our cheques. You must have debited our account by mistake.

Woman: I'm very sorry about that, Mr Bliss. I'll sort it out immediately. Could I just . . .

[pause]

Now listen to the recording again.

[pause]

Conversation 3. Questions 9–12.

Look at the note below.

You will hear a woman calling about a conference booking.

You have 15 seconds to read through the notes.

[pause]

Now listen, and fill in the spaces.

Woman 1: Good morning. Rachel Bould's office. Can I help you?

Woman 2: Good morning. This is Janet Shibuya here, from the Conference Reservation Service. Can I speak to Rachel?

Woman 1: I'm afraid she's out of the office. Would you like to leave a message?

Woman 2: Sure. I just wanted to update her on the booking for your Management Seminar on the 24th of April.

Woman 1: Oh yes. At the Russell Hotel.

Woman 2: Well, no, that's what I'm phoning about. I wasn't able to get the Russell Hotel, they were fully booked. But I've got you in at the Tower Hotel. That's in the centre of London too, the location's very convenient.

Woman 1: And what about the price?

Woman 2: Well, the basic price is the same. The good thing is that now you have the choice of a buffet lunch or a full restaurant meal. The buffet lunch is cheaper, so would you like to go for that?

Woman 1: I'll ask Mrs Bould about that and let you know.

Woman 2: Right. Then the other thing is, could you send me a list of the equipment you'll be needing – OHP, video . . . that sort of thing.

Woman 1: Can we get back to you on that one by Friday?

Woman 2: That'll be fine.

[pause]

Now listen to the recording again.

[pause]

That is the end of Part One. You now have 20 seconds to check your answers.

[pause]

Part Two. Questions 13–22.

Section 1. Questions 13–17.

You will hear five short recordings. The five speakers are explaining what their jobs involve.

For each recording, decide what the speaker's job is.

Write one letter (A–H) next to the number of the recording.

Do not use any letter more than once.

After you have listened once, replay each recording.

You have 15 seconds to read the list A–H.

[pause]

Now listen, and decide what each speaker's job is.

[pause]

Thirteen

Man: I have monthly targets set by head office. Now, customers usually need a lot of help choosing the right product, which is fair enough, but at the same time I've got to make sure that what I do is cost-effective for the company, so I have to watch my time and expenses carefully.

[pause]

Fourteen

Man: The interesting part of the job is the staff development side – arranging training and organising appraisals. And we're doing more of that because more training time is necessary to keep staff up-to-date with computer applications. It's nice to do this as a change

from the routine of advertising, interviewing, drawing up staff contracts, etc.

[pause]

Fifteen

Woman: The company's got cashflow difficulties at present – the problem lies with our larger customers. They've been delaying payments and we are in danger of going into the red. I'm negotiating with these clients to find a solution. If I don't succeed, we may not be able to pay our own bills!

[pause]

Sixteen

Man: I'm responsible for making sure that our stock levels are sufficient to meet orders. Customers don't want to know about staff or technical problems – they want their goods on time. Sometimes I have to persuade staff to do overtime or hire extra machines to meet deadlines. Anything to make sure our customers get their orders.

[pause]

Seventeen

Woman: In a small insurance firm like ours, my job involves everything from completing the paperwork for policies to paying people and managing petty cash. At present I'm arranging for a new computer system to be installed, but as you'd probably expect, I do many different things.

[pause]

Section 2. Questions 18–22

You will hear another five recordings. Each speaker is describing a problem within a company.

For each recording, decide in which area there is a problem.

Write one letter (A–H) next to the number of the recording.

Do not use any letter more than once.

After you have listened once, replay each recording.

You have 15 seconds to read the list A–H.

[pause]

Now listen, and decide in which area each problem is.

[pause]

Eighteen

Man: We've been getting cancellations of orders from clients, saying they've been receiving faulty goods. We need to improve the system – random checking isn't good enough any more. And sales team leaders need to watch the situation carefully and report cancellations to head office immediately.

[pause]

Nineteen

Woman: I've been trying to find ways of increasing production. I've introduced new shifts and production targets. But at the end of the day, we're limited by a constant manpower shortage. Last month three of our best people left us because of bad working relationships. It's clear that, unless we can keep trained staff, our production problems won't go away.

[pause]

Twenty

Man: Well, in our latest market research exercise, we looked at things like advertising, publicity, customer services. And we got a lot of complaints, especially about our information desks. It also seems that we are not really getting our message across to the media properly – we need to manage that better too.

[pause]

Twenty-one

Woman: Finally, I believe that we need to create new departments and set departmental targets to direct our work. This will reduce inefficiency and increase output. The company has grown very quickly, in many directions, and it's time to work in a more systematic way.

[pause]

Twenty-two

Woman: We're getting complaints about the quality of work on the shop-floor. But for us, the problem lies with what's happening with supervisors and section heads. When we take problems or suggestions to supervisors, they often don't go any further. And information from above isn't reaching us on the shop-floor.

[pause]

That is the end of Part Two.

[pause]

Part Three. Questions 23–30.

You will hear a radio interview with the Managing Director of a restaurant chain.

For each question 23–30, mark one letter (A, B or C) for the correct answer.

After you have listened once, replay the recording.

You have 45 seconds to read through the questions.

[pause]

Now listen, and mark A, B or C.

[pause]

Man: I have in the studio with me today Olivia Peyton, who set up the Pacific Bar & Grill with her brother Tom in 1994, when she was 30. They now have a restaurant chain with a £20 million turnover. Olivia, what gave you the drive to achieve so much at such a young age?

Woman: Well, our parents taught us the important lesson that you should never be afraid of failure. But really, it was when we moved to England from Australia when I was a teenager. I felt like an outsider, because of my accent and interests, so that gave me a strong desire to do better at school than those who'd always lived here. I felt the need to be educated. I was more likely to take chances . . .

Man: You didn't study catering at university though, did you?

Woman: No. I'd never thought of that as a career. I studied English Literature. My parents tried to persuade me to take up a career in finance – my best exam results at school were in Maths. So they were disappointed when I did Literature . . . but I wanted to be a writer regardless of whether I could write! I didn't do fantastically well in my degree, though.

Man: So, what do you think has made you successful as a businesswoman? What is it that makes someone able to progress as an entrepreneur in the business world?

Woman: Well, in my case, I think it's more a reflection of my mental capacity than all the books I've read and the skills I learnt at university. I mean I can write a good letter now but that isn't going to make me successful. But I've got a fundamental understanding of business. I can see very easily in my mind how things are going to go.

Man: OK. Let's move on now to talk about your career. First, you got into the soft drinks business . . .

Woman: Yes . . . in the late eighties. But we soon found that importing drinks is a bit of a dull business – nothing much was happening, so we sold up in 1991 and thought 'What shall we do now?' We decided to go travelling for a year, but we wanted to work while travelling. Then when we were in Australia, we met someone in the drinks industry who had a chain of restaurants there. He took us on. My brother was a waiter and I was working in the office, doing a lot of the day-to-day running of the restaurant, and in doing that I learnt the basics, such as what to buy, how many chefs to employ and so on.

Man: And you stayed there until 1994.

Woman: Yes, then we came back here and started the Pacific Grill straight away.

Man: You and your brother must be a good team.

Woman: Well, Tom and I always discuss things but he's more creative and comes up with all the ideas while I look after the business side. The thing about working with family is that you know they're going to be there tomorrow. You can employ other key people, but then if you upset them, they'll probably leave.

Man: Sure. People say it's tough work.

Woman: There's no doubt that it is. Some staff don't go home until 4.30 in the morning . . . but then they might not be on until the next evening. I only work during the day I might add! I like to have some time to myself but most people in the restaurant business aren't like me. People in the business tend to be outgoing, sociable types – the sort who enjoy an environment of constant activity and tight deadlines.

Man: What would you say to anyone who's thinking of going into the catering business?

Woman: I'd say, start at the bottom. Interestingly, one of the institutions here is developing a recruitment technique based not on degrees and work experience but on the ability to learn. The food industry still maintains the idea of apprenticeship. Running a restaurant, working with the public – these are very complex skills and you must be prepared to start at the bottom and learn quickly.

Man: Well, thank you for coming along to the studio today, Olivia, and I wish you every success . . .

[pause]

Now listen to the recording again.

[pause]

That is the end of Part Three. You now have ten minutes to transfer your answers to your Answer Sheet. Stop here and time ten minutes.

INTERLOCUTOR FRAMES

To facilitate practice for the Speaking test, the scripts followed by the interlocutor for Parts 2 and 3 appear below. They should be used in conjunction with Tests 1–4 Speaking tasks.

Interlocutor frames are not included for Part 1, in which the interlocutor asks the candidates questions directly rather than asking them to perform tasks.

PART 2: Mini presentations for 2 candidates (about 6 minutes)

Interlocutor:
- I'm going to give each of you a choice of 3 topics. I'd like you to choose one of the topics and give a short presentation on it for about a minute. You will have about a minute to prepare for this and you can make notes if you wish while you prepare. After you have finished your talk, your partner will ask you a question.
- All right? Here are your topics.

[Interlocutor hands each candidate a different topic card, and some paper and a pencil for notes.]

Interlocutor:
- Choose one of the topics to talk about. You can make notes.

[1 minute's preparation time. Both candidates prepare their talks at the same time, separately.]

Interlocutor:
- All right. Now, *B, which topic have you chosen, A, B or C? Would you like to talk about what you think is important when (xxx).

[B talks.]

Interlocutor:
- Thank you. Now, *A, please ask *B your question about his/her talk.

[A asks question.]

Interlocutor:
- Thank you. All right. Now, *A, which topic have you chosen, A, B or C? would you like to talk about what you think is important when (xxx).

[A talks.]

Interlocutor:
- Thank you. Now, *B, please ask *A your question about his/her talk.

[B asks question.]

Interlocutor:
- Thank you.

[Materials are collected.]

*USE CANDIDATES' NAMES THROUGHOUT THE TEST

PART 3 : Collaborative task and discussion (about 5 minutes)

Interlocutor:
- Now this part of the test you are going to discuss together.

[Interlocutor points to the card showing the task while giving the instructions below.]

Interlocutor:
- You have 30 seconds to read the task carefully, and then 3 minutes to discuss and decide about it together. You should give reasons for your decisions and opinions. You don't need to write anything. Is that clear?

[Interlocutor places the card in front of the candidates.]

Interlocutor:
- I'm just going to listen and then ask you to stop after about 3 minutes. Please speak so that we can hear you.

[Candidates have about 3 minutes to complete the task.]

[Materials are collected.]

[The Interlocutor asks one or more of the following questions as appropriate, to extend the discussion.]

Example:
- What kinds of information about your company would you give to members of a foreign trade delegation? (Why?)

Interlocutor frames

- Is socialising with clients an important part of business? (Why/Why not?)
- If you were invited to attend a foreign trade delegation, which country would you most like to visit? (Why?)
- How can companies increase their international contacts?

- Do you think business will become more global in the future? (Why/Why not?)
- Do you think English will continue to be the most widely used language in international business? (Why/Why not?)

- Thank you. That is the end of the Speaking Test.

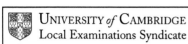
UNIVERSITY *of* CAMBRIDGE
Local Examinations Syndicate

V A N T A G E

Candidate Name
If not already printed, write name
in CAPITALS and complete the
Candidate No. grid (in pencil).

Candidate's Signature

Examination Title

Centre

Supervisor:
If the candidate is ABSENT or has WITHDRAWN shade here ⊐

Centre No.

Candidate No.

**Examination
Details**

0	0	0	0
1	1	1	1
2	2	2	2
3	3	3	3
4	4	4	4
5	5	5	5
6	6	6	6
7	7	7	7
8	8	8	8
9	9	9	9

BEC Vantage Reading Answer Sheet

Instructions
Use a PENCIL (B or HB).
Rub out any answer you wish to change with an eraser.

For **Parts 1 to 4**:
Mark one box for each answer.

For example:
If you think C is the right answer to the question, mark your answer sheet like this:

0   A   B   C

For **Part 5**:
Write your answer clearly in CAPITAL LETTERS.
Write one letter in each box.

For example:

0 E N G L I S H

Part 1

1	A	B	C	D
2	A	B	C	D
3	A	B	C	D
4	A	B	C	D
5	A	B	C	D
6	A	B	C	D
7	A	B	C	D

Part 2

8	A	B	C	D	E	F	G
9	A	B	C	D	E	F	G
10	A	B	C	D	E	F	G
11	A	B	C	D	E	F	G
12	A	B	C	D	E	F	G

Turn over for Parts 3 - 5 ▶

BEC V - R

DP458/358

Photocopiable © UCLES

Part 3

13	A	B	C	D
14	A	B	C	D
15	A	B	C	D
16	A	B	C	D
17	A	B	C	D
18	A	B	C	D

Part 4

19	A	B	C	D
20	A	B	C	D
21	A	B	C	D
22	A	B	C	D
23	A	B	C	D
24	A	B	C	D
25	A	B	C	D
26	A	B	C	D

27	A	B	C	D
28	A	B	C	D
29	A	B	C	D
30	A	B	C	D
31	A	B	C	D
32	A	B	C	D
33	A	B	C	D

Part 5

34		1 34 0
35		1 35 0
36		1 36 0
37		1 37 0
38		1 38 0
39		1 39 0
40		1 40 0
41		1 41 0
42		1 42 0
43		1 43 0
44		1 44 0
45		1 45 0

Photocopiable © UCLES

UNIVERSITY *of* CAMBRIDGE
Local Examinations Syndicate

V A N T A G E

Candidate Name
If not already printed, write name
in CAPITALS and complete the
Candidate No. grid (in pencil).

Candidate's Signature

Examination Title

Centre

Supervisor:

If the candidate is ABSENT or has WITHDRAWN shade here ▭

Centre No.

Candidate No.

Examination Details

0	0	0	0
1	1	1	1
2	2	2	2
3	3	3	3
4	4	4	4
5	5	5	5
6	6	6	6
7	7	7	7
8	8	8	8
9	9	9	9

BEC Vantage Listening Answer Sheet

Instructions
Use a PENCIL (B or HB).
Rub out any answer you wish to change with an eraser.

For **Part 1:**
Write your answer clearly in CAPITAL LETTERS.
Write one letter or number in each box.
If the answer has more than one word, leave one box empty between words.

For example:

0 | Q U E S T I O N | 1 2

For **Parts 2 and 3:**
Mark one box for each answer.

For example:
If you think C is the right answer to the question, mark your answer sheet like this:

0 | A B C

Part 1 - Conversation One

1 | | 1 1 0

2 | | 1 2 0

3 | | 1 3 0

4 | | 1 4 0

Continue on the other side of this sheet ▶

BEC V - L   DP460/360

Photocopiable © UCLES

121

Part 1 - Conversation Two

5 ⟨ ⟩ 1 5 0

6 ⟨ ⟩ 1 6 0

7 ⟨ ⟩ 1 7 0

8 ⟨ ⟩ 1 8 0

Part 1 - Conversation Three

9 ⟨ ⟩ 1 9 0

10 ⟨ ⟩ 1 10 0

11 ⟨ ⟩ 1 11 0

12 ⟨ ⟩ 1 12 0

Part 2 - Section One

	A	B	C	D	E	F	G	H
13	A	B	C	D	E	F	G	H
14	A	B	C	D	E	F	G	H
15	A	B	C	D	E	F	G	H
16	A	B	C	D	E	F	G	H
17	A	B	C	D	E	F	G	H

Part 2 - Section Two

	A	B	C	D	E	F	G	H
18	A	B	C	D	E	F	G	H
19	A	B	C	D	E	F	G	H
20	A	B	C	D	E	F	G	H
21	A	B	C	D	E	F	G	H
22	A	B	C	D	E	F	G	H

Part 3

	A	B	C
23	A	B	C
24	A	B	C
25	A	B	C
26	A	B	C
27	A	B	C
28	A	B	C
29	A	B	C
30	A	B	C

Photocopiable © UCLES

122

Thanks and acknowledgements

The authors and publishers are grateful to the following copyright owners for permission to reproduce copyright material. Every endeavour has been made to contact holders and apologies are expressed for any omissions.

p. 42 © Telegraph Group Limited 2000; p. 60 *Strategy in Crisis* by Michael de Kare-Silver © Macmillan, London; p. 62 by Hester Lacey © The Independent/Syndication, 12/9/99; p. 66 by Stuart Crainer, *The Real Power of Brands*, Pitman Publishing 1995; p. 79 Management Publications Ltd; p. 80 by Rodney Hobson © Times Newspapers Limited, 22/03/96; p. 82 by Rupert Merson © The Independent/Syndication, 27/6/99; p. 84 © Ian Marcouse and David Lines, reprinted by permission of Pearson Education Limited; p. 86 *Teach Yourself Time Management* by Polly Bird. Reproduced by permission of Hodder and Stoughton Educational Limited.

Lightning Source UK Ltd.
Milton Keynes UK
UKOW02f1439190713

213994UK00005B/77/P